DEVANEY

A DYNASTY REMEMBERED

Jerry Tagge's Scrapbook
History of the Nebraska Cornhuskers'
Greatest Football Era

Edited by
Francis J. Fitzgerald
and
Jerry Tagge

Athlon
Nashville, Tennessee

Portions of this book have been previously published. Listed below is their original source of publication:

Chapters 1, 8, 9, 13, 14, 17, 18, 19, 20, 22, 28, 29, 30, 31 and 32 have been previously published in *The Omaha World Herald*. Reprinted by permission of The Omaha World Herald.

Chapters 4, 11, 15, 34, 42 and 56 have been previously published by United Press International. Reprinted by permission of United Press International.

Chapters 7, 10, 21, 23, 24 and 62 have been previously published by The Associated Press. Reprinted by permission of The Associated Press.

Chapters 33, 39, 43, 45 and 63 have been previously published in *The Miami Herald*. Reprinted by permission of The Miami Herald/Knight-Ridder Newspapers Inc.

Chapters 35 and 36 have been previously published in *The Dallas Morning News*. Reprinted by permission of The Dallas Morning News.

Chapter 37 has been previously published in *Newsweek*. Reprinted by permission of Newsweek.

Chapter 38 has been previously published in *Time*. Reprinted by permission of Time Inc.

Chapters 40, 46, 48, 49, 53, 57 and 59 have been previously published in *Sports Illustrated*. Reprinted by permission of Time Inc.

Chapter 41 has been previously published in *The New Orleans Times*. Reprinted by permission of The New Orleans Times-Picayune.

Chapters 47, 50, 51, 52, 54, 55, 58, 60, 61 and 64 have been previously published in *The New York Times*. Reprinted by permission of The New York Times Company.

Chapter 65 has been previously published in the book *College Football's 25 Greatest Teams*. Reprinted by permission of The Sporting News.

Published by
Athlon Sports Communications
220 25th Avenue North
Nashville, Tennessee 37203

"EVEN THE POPE WOULD HAVE TO
VOTE US NO. 1."

— *Bob Devaney*

Contents

INTRODUCTION

On a very warm New Year's Day 1973 evening in a jam-packed Miami's Orange Bowl Stadium, a massive throng of over 35,000 Big Red rooters unleashed nearly three decades of pent-up frustrations and claimed their right to the throne which rules over the rest of the college football world. It was an evening to remember and savor.

This emotional outpouring began to take shape when Bob Devaney's Nebraska Cornhusker football team, who had been crowned as national champions for the past two seasons and was now sporting an 8-2-1 record, had come to Miami to battle Ara Parseghian's Notre Dame powerhouse. The game was to be Devaney's finale as the coach of Nebraska, thus bringing an end to an 11-year run that had rewritten the history of Cornhusker football. Together, he and his teams had built a dynasty that few will ever match.

With a halftime lead of 20-0, Johnny Rodgers, the Heisman Memorial Trophy winner, began a personal assault on the end-zone scoreboard. Having already rushed and passed for pair of touchdowns in the first half, Rodgers came back in the third quarter and scored three more touchdowns in a span of 6 minutes 43 seconds. It was a display of football talent that had rarely been exhibited before.

Rodgers' final touchdown was the spark that pushed the mania of Big Red fans to a new level of ecstacy. Having taken a short pass from Cornhusker quarterback David Humm near the midfield sideline, the fleet-footed halfback danced his way past weary and frustrated Notre Dame tacklers and on towards the end zone. With each yard that Rodgers traveled, the Orange Bowl crowd's chanting and screaming grew to new heights. And when he crossed the goal line, the fevered pitch exploded into sheer pandemonium.

For the Nebraska football faithful it would never get any better than this.

To understand how this Orange Bowl fireworks display had pushed the Cornhusker fans to such dizzily emotional heights, one must understand the history of the University of Nebraska football program. It is a history which has had scattered flirtations with success, but never enjoyed continuous prosperity. Long overshadowed by its rival, the University of Oklahoma Sooners, and rarely able to make much of a mark on the national scene, the Cornhuskers had been trying for decades to find its place among the college football elite.

In the era of Fred Dawson's coaching reign, the Cornhuskers took on and slayed Knute Rockne's fabled Four Horsemen teams of 1922 and 1923. Then later, in Biff Jones' tenure, the former coach of the powerhouse Army teams took his Nebraska squad west to play in the 1941 Rose Bowl against Marchy Schwartz's Stanford Indians. Unfortunately, the Cornhuskers lost that contest. Afterwards, a long dry spell hit the Nebraska football program and there would be little to cheer about for more than 20 years.

During this time most Cornhusker fans switched their allegiance to follow a Nebraska-raised lad by the name of Frank Leahy who had played for Knute Rockne at Notre Dame in the late 1920's and had returned to his alma mater in 1941. Leahy's teams were the toast of football fans from coast to coast. In his 11-year tenure at Notre Dame, which covered a 13-year period that was briefly interrupted by World War II, Leahy's Irish Football Machine won five national championships, fielded six undefeated teams and amassed an 87-11-9 record. He also had four Heisman Trophy winners and 29 all-America players. National radio and television audiences each autumn Saturday afternoon tuned in to the epic battles being waged by Leahy's great teams.

With little to cheer about, large doses of the Cornhusker faithful became part of the ever-growing congregation who converted and began to cheer for Leahy's Fighting Irish. However, in 1962, something important happened to halt this mass exodus.

The Nebraska football program, which was in great need of a savior, found an unlikely candidate by the name of Robert S. Devaney, who had enjoyed considerable success at the nearby outpost of the college football world, Wyoming U. Devaney was quickly hired to breathe new life into a proud school that was searching for the road to big-time football.

In his first season, Devaney turned the anemic Cornhusker program around and posted a 9-2 record. But even with this newfound success, the Cornhusker faithful held their breath.

After going 9-2 in the regular season and accepting the Gotham Bowl bid, some problems involving the Gotham Bowl's financial guarantee to each team cropped up. Certain administrative officials from both schools, Miami and Nebraska, threatened to hold their teams out of the bowl game unless the financial guarantees could be straightened out prior to the game.

Finally, Robert Wagner, the Mayor of New York City, stepped in on Thursday, December 13 — just two days before the game — and guaranteed traveling expenses of $30,000 for Miami and $35,000 for Nebraska. Miami athletic officials quickly accepted the plan but Nebraska officials wanted something more secure. They demanded payment in hand.

When issued a check for $35,000 on late Thursday afternoon, the Nebraska athletic ticket manager, Jim Pittenger, who was in New York clearing local logistics for the bowl game, was told by University of Nebraska officials to make sure that the funds for the check were good before they would allow the football team to depart the next morning, on Friday, for New York City.

With the banks in New York City opening at 10 A.M., Pittenger met with bowl officials at the headquarters of Bankers Trust in Manhattan shortly after the bank began its morning business.

Back in Lincoln, Neb., an assembled Nebraska football team and school officials who had been waiting for several hours at the Lincoln Airport — all dressed to travel with bags packed — huddled around Dye and Nebraska football coach Bob Devaney to learn of the results of the long-awaited telephone call.

At 8:30, Pittenger's call rang through. Matter of factly, he proceeded to explain, "Yes, the check had cleared."

It was at this point that Devaney began to beam. Speaking with great emotion he proclaimed: "All right, we've been waiting a long time to get on these airplanes, now let's get on 'em."

A wild display of whooping and hollering quickly erupted as the team and school officials rushed for the planes.

In a way, Devaney's miraculous turnaround of the Nebraska football program had been too much, too quick. Cornhusker fans must have thought it a mirage. They had desperately wanted to believe in what was happening, but something was holding them back.

More importantly, the University of Nebraska's handling of the Gotham Bowl's guarantee, which had been backed by the Mayor of New York City, proved they, too, thought that all of the success of Devaney's dream season was a bubble that could still be quickly burst.

Yet when Devaney's team boarded those two airplanes that cold December day in Lincoln, they weren't just headed for New York City. Instead, it was only the first step on an 11-year whirlwind that would take the Nebraska Cornhuskers to the top of the college football world. And after the journey was over, Devaney and his teams had built a dynasty that only a few schools could ever boast of.

Eventually, those who had doubted the Devaney miracle were converted. Nebraska beat a heavily favored Miami Hurricanes squad in a wild shootout, 36-34, in the Gotham Bowl that next day. They then went on to play against and beat most of the nation's top teams for the next decade.

Suddenly, Devaney & Co. were in vogue. They began to take trips to New Orleans and Dallas to play in the Sugar Bowl and the Cotton Bowl. The Cornhuskers were in the Orange Bowl so often during Devaney's reign that Miami, Fla., seemed like their winter home.

There would be Big Eight Conference Championships in 1963, '64, '65, '66, '69, '70, '71 and 72. And the back-to-back national championships in 1970 and 1971.

Finally, on New Year's Day evening in 1973, fate traveled full circle.

In this game, Devaney's last as coach of the Cornhuskers, his Big Red team was coming head-to-head with the school whose storied teams while under the reign of Frank Leahy had stolen Nebraska's fans and a part of their past tradition. Prior to the 1973 Orange Bowl game, a large number of Nebraska rooters had made amends for their long-ago sins of having deserted the Cornhusker teams of the 1940's and 50's. But on this special evening, these past indifferences were put aside and the Nebraska faithful all came together and fervently cheered their team on to a 40-6 rout of the Fighting Irish.

It was a magical night that will be long remembered.

This book, "Devaney: A Dynasty Remembered," is a sentimental trip into yesteryear which brings to life and celebrates Bob Devaney's great era at the helm of the Nebraska Cornhusker football steamroller. It is a collection of the best stories ever written on this 11-year journey to both glory and triumph. These stories were chronicled by the best sports writers in America.

"Devaney: A Dynasty Remembered" takes you back to those memorable days when a school, a state and its football fans were in search of their past and in the process discovered the destiny of their future. It is also a story of a guy named Bob Devaney who led the Nebraska football faithful to find their place in the sun, where they were able to bask in its wonderful warmth.

Francis J. Fitzgerald
Washington, D.C.
July 14, 1994

THE COURTING
OF A SAVIOR

1

Nebraska To Name Devaney On Saturday?

By GREGG McBRIDE
Special to The Omaha World-Herald

LOS ANGELES, Calif., January 3, 1962 — Rose Bowl writers expressed interest in the University of Nebraska football situation.

"The Cornhuskers have missed the boat since before World War II, and I suppose they are going to make their usual blunder," observed an occupant of the Rose Bowl's new press coop.

But there was one real hot tip which came from the Rocky Mountain region.

This was that Wyoming's Coach Bob Devaney is the new Cornhusker mentor and his selection will be announced Saturday.

The Cowboy mentor's shift to Lincoln hinges merely on whether he can get his release from Wyoming.

Chester Nelson, *The Rocky Mountain News* sports editor, was my Pasadena information source. He claims a pipeline direct from Laramie.

The redhead's report came on the heels of a similar tip from Wiles Hallock, the University of California sports information director. Hallock was the Cowboy press agent before joining the Bears.

Another choice bit of information gleaned from the Pasadena pow-wow includes that Bill Barnes, the coach of U.C.L.A.'s Pacific Coast champions, can be had for Nebraska if properly approached.

Paul Zimmerman, *The Los Angeles Times* sports editor and a former Cornhusker track athlete, had the information on Barnes.

The *Times* sports editor says he has reason to believe Barnes is "definitely interested in Nebraska."

The Bruin mentor, looking toward the future, is concerned over a trend at U.C.L.A. to step up scholastic requirements.

Barnes has finished his seventeenth coaching season. He started as a freshman assistant at Tennessee, his alma mater, was four years on the Arkansas staff, then joined U.C.L.A. in 1950.

In three seasons as head man with the Bruins, Barnes has enjoyed three winning campaigns. His 19-10-2 record includes a tie with Washington for the 1959 Big Five championship and the undisputed championship last fall.

2

Devaney, Wyoming Talks Due

From WORLD-HERALD WIRE SERVICES
The Omaha World-Herald

OMAHA, Neb., January 4, 1962 — A showdown is expected today or Friday in the cowboy town of Laramie, Wyo.

This won't be the type prevalent when the West was young. It concerns the likely request of Wyoming Football Coach Bob Devaney to break his contract to accept a similar position at Nebraska.

Cowboy Athletic Director Glenn Jacoby said Wednesday he hopes to start talks today or Friday with Devaney, who is due back on the campus after attending the Sugar Bowl game in New Orleans, La.

"The first thing to do is find out if there's to be any vacancy," Jacoby told The Associated Press. "It's silly to be talking about replacements now."

Jacoby said he had talked with Devaney several times within the past week "but it's pretty difficult to do this over the phone.

"Until we do talk with Bob, I think it would be very unfair to Bob or to us to say anything about the contract," Jacoby told United Press International. He said he was afraid it might get the meeting with Devaney off on the wrong foot.

Speculation that Devaney will get the Nebraska job was strengthened by a report from Salt Lake City that both Utah's Ray Nagel and Utah State's John Ralston feel they are out of the running.

Nagel and Ralston told *Salt Lake Tribune* sports editor John Mooney they have had no further contacts since interviewed by Tippy Dye, the former Wichita State University athletic director who recently occupied a similar position at Nebraska.

Devaney is the only one of the three to talk to the Nebraska regents, Mooney said, and the only one to visit the Cornhusker campus.

Both Nagel and Ralston told Mooney they thought Devaney was Nebraska's choice.

In Wichita, Dye said if a contract agreement is reached with the man he has in mind the Nebraska job could be filled this weekend.

"If not," Dye added, "it could be a very long time."

If Devaney is the man, trouble may lie ahead.

A source close to the Wyoming situation said the school has no intention of letting Devaney go, especially since he signed a new five-year contract last summer after asking for more security.

"Wyoming will live up to its bargain and expects Devaney to honor his obligation," the source said.

Wyoming newsmen offered these observations:

— Devaney is cooling toward the Nebraska job and Utah's Nagel has been called for another interview with Husker officials.

— Devaney wants more money than Nebraska is willing to pay. It was reported Devaney is making $16,000 a year at Wyoming and has a rent-free house.

— Devaney might stay at Wyoming to await an opening at Michigan State, where he formerly was an assistant coach.

— Devaney will move to Nebraska to gain more prestige while still keeping an eye on a future Michigan State post.

Dye said he will leave Wichita today for Lincoln, then go next week to the N.C.A.A. convention in Chicago. Mrs. Dye said the family's move is scheduled about January 20.

3

Devaney Poised To Accept N.U. Job, If Cowboys Agree

From WORLD-HERALD WIRE SERVICES
The Omaha World-Herald

OMAHA, Neb., January 5, 1962 — All that's needed to solve the University of Nebraska coaching puzzle is a nod from Bob Devaney.

Devaney, the successful University of Wyoming mentor, on Thursday was reported eager to accept the Cornhusker appointment.

All he needs is to pry himself loose from his Wyoming contract.

If successful in obtaining his release, Devaney's choice as successor to Bill Jennings is expected to be confirmed during a meeting of the Nebraska Board of Regents on Saturday.

The regents at the time also are expected to reveal the salary of Tippy Dye, the former Wichita State University athletic director, who has taken over as Cornhusker athletic director.

The World-Herald learned Dye will receive about $17,000 in salary.

If Devaney is unable to spring himself from Laramie, then Ray Nagel, the University of Utah coach, is said to be in line.

John Ralston, the Utah State coach who was an early candidate, is said to be out of the picture.

A late entry, Bill Barnes of U.C.L.A.'s Rose Bowl team, is available and could get the nod as third choice behind Devaney and Nagel.

4

Devaney Asks Wyoming For Release To Become Nebraska Grid Coach

By UNITED PRESS INTERNATIONAL
The New York Times

LARAMIE, Wyo., January 6, 1962 — Wyoming's football coach, Robert S. (Bob) Devaney, formally asked today for waiver of his contract so he could accept the head coaching job at the University of Nebraska.

Devaney's request to take the Cornhusker post was announced by the Cowboys' athletic director, Glenn (Red) Jacoby. Jacoby said the matter is now out of the hands of both himself and G. D. Humphrey, the president of the University of Wyoming.

"We do not have the power to grant the release ourselves," Jacoby said. "Only the board of trustees can do it."

'Up to Wyoming board'

He said the matter now was "up to the Nebraska Board of Regents and the (Wyoming) trustees. If Nebraska insists, the Wyoming board will have to release him. It is up to the Wyoming board now."

Devaney signed a new contract with the University of Wyoming last summer. It was reported that the contract still had four years and nine months to run.

At Lincoln, the Nebraska athletic director, Tippy Dye, said Devaney "has been and still is our No. 1 choice for head football coach."

Devaney would replace Bill Jennings, whose contract was not renewed after last season.

Nebraska Regents Meet

The Nebraska regents met in Lincoln today to discuss hiring

Devaney, but adjourned the meeting without making an official announcement. However, the board authorized Dye and the chancellor of the university, Clifford Hardin, to get in touch with Wyoming officials to try to arrange the waiver of Devaney's contract.

Members of the Wyoming Board of Trustees expressed deep disappointment at Devaney's choice. There did not appear to be a strong trend, however, concerning whether they individually favored releasing him from his contract.

There were indications in Lincoln that the Nebraska administration would await the Wyoming trustees' action before deciding on Devaney's appointment.

Wyoming's trustees are scheduled to meet Feb. 5 and 6.

Clifford P. Hansen, the chairman of the Wyoming trustees, said the board would be polled by telegram to determine its wishes regarding Devaney's request. He said the results might be made known tomorrow.

5

Board To Let Devaney Go To N.U. Post

From WORLD-HERALD WIRE SERVICES
The Omaha World-Herald

OMAHA, Neb., January 6, 1962 — The University of Wyoming Board of Trustees is willing to permit Football Coach Bob Devaney to take a similar post at Nebraska, *The Wyoming Eagle* said Friday.

"A well-informed source said an informal telephone poll of University of Wyoming board members revealed that the board . . . (is) in favor of allowing Devaney to be free from his contract obligations so he can accept the Nebraska job," United Press International quoted the Cheyenne newspaper as saying.

Neither Devaney nor Husker Athletic Director Tippy Dye would say so Friday, however.

Devaney said in Laramie he has made no definite decision.

Following a talk with Wyoming Athletic Director Glenn (Red) Jacoby, Devaney told The Associated Press:

"The people at Nebraska meet this weekend to decide what they want to do. If they make an offer then I will have to make up my mind and then I'd have to get a release from Wyoming."

Devaney, just back from a trip to the South, didn't consider his meeting with Jacoby a conference.

"We just talked. I haven't seen Red in quite a while," the most successful coach in Wyoming history said.

Asked if he was still interested in the Cornhusker position, Devaney answered: "Oh, yes, I'm still interested."

Thus there appears to be only a 50-50 chance that the new Nebraska coach will be announced today after a morning meeting of the Board of Regents.

Athletic Director Dye said he will talk the coaching matter over with Chancellor Clifford M. Hardin before the regents meeting."

Devaney has won or shared a Skyline Conference title in four of his five years at Wyoming. His overall record is 35-10-5 while his conference standard is 27-4-3.

6

Devaney's Release To Accept Post Expected Today

From WORLD-HERALD WIRE SERVICES
The Omaha World-Herald

OMAHA, Neb., January 7, 1962 — Robert S. Devaney is expected to be given a release today from the remaining four years on his University of Wyoming football coaching contract to accept the Nebraska grid reins.

Wyoming University President G. D. Humphrey announced Saturday night that a poll of the Wyoming Board of Trustees was being conducted to consider Devaney's request for a contract release.

President Humphrey said an announcement probably would be made today by Clifford P. Hansen, the chairman of the trustees.

A check of the Wyoming Board of Trustees indicated that although disappointed in Devaney's decision, it would release him, United Press International reported.

However, Hansen said there seems to be a "stiffening resistance" in the board against waiving long contracts.

At Laramie, The Associated Press said only formalities appeared to delay the formal announcement on Devaney's shift.

The A.P. story quoted Wyoming Athletic Director Glenn J. Jacoby: "We are quite sure the release will be granted but we can't speak for the trustees."

The formal release, Jacoby said, probably won't be granted until the trustees meet on February 2 but added there is a possibility an "unofficial understanding might be reached."

The Nebraska Board of Regents on Saturday gave Chancellor Clifford Hardin and Athletic Director Tippy Dye full power to sign Devaney when the Cowboys mentor receives his release.

The personable Devaney, whose five years at Wyoming brought

the Cowboys four Skyline Conference football titles, acknowledged he wants the job at Nebraska.

"If they will release me, I'm going to go," Devaney said.

"It wasn't an easy decision. The situation here (Wyoming) has been good but the overall factor is Nebraska has greater potential. I think the opportunities for the future are better."

Devaney was given a five-year extension on his contract at Wyoming last summer.

The 46-year-old Devaney came to Wyoming in 1957 after three years as end coach under Michigan State's Duffy Daugherty.

Before going to Michigan State, Devaney had 14 years coaching experience at Michigan high schools.

Devaney was captain of the Alma (Mich.) College team in 1938.

While at Wyoming he turned down offers for the head coaching job at Maryland and California, before deciding to make the switch to Nebraska.

The Devaneys have two children — Michael, 20, and Patricia, 17.

At Wyoming, Devaney installed the Michigan State multiple offense system, while winning 35, losing 10 and tying 5.

Three of Devaney's assistance coaches — backfield coach Mike Corgan, end coach Jim Ross and defensive line coach Lloyd Eaton — were brought to Wyoming from small colleges or high schools in Michigan.

Devaney said he has invited all his assistants to go to Nebraska. He said Ross will definitely go.

Devaney also said three members of his staff are interested in the Wyoming coaching job. But he added it would not be fair to say who they were or which one he considered best qualified.

After trying unsuccessfully to receive Devaney's release by telephone, Dye released this statement:

"Out of respect for the Board of Trustees at the University of Wyoming, no official action will be taken at this time and no formal recommendation has been made by the University of Nebraska board."

At a press conference after attempts to obtain Devaney's release for a formal announcement broke down, Dye divulged that he has known Devaney only three weeks — about the length of time of negotiations.

At least as far as the regents were concerned Dye didn't go away exactly empty-handed.

The board approved Dye's appointment at an annual salary of $18,500 and gave him a vote of "full confidence that the intercollegiate program will move forward on a sound basis under his leadership."

The salary placed Dye in a bracket considerably higher than the Governor of Nebraska ($14,000) but not on the same level with Chancellor Hardin.

There was no discussion on the salary negotiations with Devaney, who will replace Bill Jennings as Husker boss. Jennings, who signed as backfield coach at Kansas last week, coached five years in Nebraska.

7

Devaney Poll Incomplete

By THE ASSOCIATED PRESS
The Omaha World-Herald

LARAMIE, Wyo., January 8, 1962 — The formality of releasing Wyoming University Football Coach Bob Devaney from his contract is expected to be completed today, a spokesman said Sunday night.

A telegraphic poll is being conducted of the 12 members of the Board of Trustees. Director of Athletics Glenn Jacoby said because of weekend absences of several trustees it would not be possible to finish the poll until today.

Jacoby said he expects the trustees to release Devaney from his contract, which has 4½ years to run, so he may sign as football coach at the University of Nebraska.

Jacoby said he is already seeking a successor to Devaney. He left for Chicago Sunday to attend the American Football Coaches Association convention, where he hopes to find a replacement.

Jacoby said he hopes to have his man by February 2.

Among those considered beside Devaney's assistant coaches are Utah State's John Ralston, Brigham Young assistant Carl Rollins and Italo Caccia, the head coach at Idaho State.

8

Action On Devaney Release Is Delayed

From WORLD-HERALD NEWS STAFF
The Omaha World-Herald

OMAHA, Neb., January 9, 1962 — Despite "serious objections" to his release from a Wyoming University contract, Football Coach Bob Devaney plans to meet with University of Nebraska football players today in Lincoln.

He is scheduled to arrive in Omaha this morning by train, then drive to Lincoln with Roy G. Holly, the dean of the Graduate School, who lives in Omaha.

Devaney plans to leave Lincoln tonight or early Wednesday morning to attend meetings of the American Football Coaches Association being held in Chicago in conjunction with the annual N.C.A.A. convention.

Assistant coach Jim Ross will accompany Devaney on the trip.

The hiring of Devaney as successor to Bill Jennings hit a snag Monday when the Wyoming Board of Trustees decided to postpone action on his request for a contract release.

Clifford P. Hansen of Jackson, Wyo., the chairman of the Wyoming board, said no decision will be made before a meeting February 2.

Devaney has been at Wyoming five years, with his teams winning or sharing four Skyline Conference championships while building a 35-10-5 record.

His contract has four years and approximately nine months to run.

In a telegram to Wyoming President Dr. G. D. Humphrey, Hansen said: "On the basis of incomplete returns from a telegraphic poll and because of serious objections of several board members, it appears that discussions concerning Devaney's release are of sufficient importance as to require more complete information and discussion at a full board meeting February 2."

Devaney said postponement of the poll was "something of a surprise."

According to United Press International, Devaney discounted a published report that he might reconsider going to Nebraska.

"It's just a matter of what the board decides to do," the coach said.

"I told the people at Nebraska I would like to go there, pending my release, and now it's up to the Wyoming trustees."

Devaney had planned to fly to Lincoln on Monday. Bad weather grounded his plane at Cheyenne.

In Chicago later this week, he will discuss his contract problems with Nebraska Athletic Director Tippy Dye, who was on hand Monday for the opening session of the N.C.A.A. convention.

Athletic Director Dye was somewhat stunned when he heard of the trustees' action.

"I don't know what we will do now," he said. "we'll just have to wait for official word from Wyoming."

Dye said he had expected Devaney's release.

Meanwhile, the Husker football office is being manned by assistant coaches Cletus Fischer, George Kelly and Jack Braley.

9

Devaney: N.U. Needs Bigger Fieldhouse

By GREGG McBRIDE
Special to The Omaha World-Herald

OMAHA, Neb., January 10, 1962 — Wyoming Coach Bob Devaney didn't hesitate to suggest changes in the University of Nebraska set-up in his visit to Lincoln Tuesday.

The man who is expected to take the Nebraska head coaching job as soon as he is released from his Wyoming contract said a bigger fieldhouse is needed if Nebraska is to keep pace in football.

Devaney said the Nebraska facilities, with the exception of Memorial Stadium, are inferior to those at Wyoming.

"This," he quickly added, "is no criticism of the Nebraska facilities, but is an honest answer to a question."

He foresees the fieldhouse being built to the south of the Stadium. He added Wyoming's modern fieldhouse has been of great benefit to the football team.

Devaney said he may drop the traditional spring Varsity-Alumni football game if he figures he can put the time to better use.

He said the alumni contest is beneficial only if the alumni can be on the campus a week and train under a coach.

Nebraska football players were favorably impressed in their first meeting with Devaney.

And Devaney liked what he saw, too.

The players said they liked the way Devaney "laid it on the line" regarding future plans.

Later, at a press conference, Devaney said the players who will man the 1962 Scarlet Machine seemed "enthusiastic, interested, polite and a fine group of boys."

He thought the current Huskers bigger than his Wyoming squad. Then he commented:

"At Wyoming we never stressed size but rather — No. 1 — desire, then team speed and quickness.

"We were not concerned with weight — just so a player weighed around two hundred pounds. And we have had success with those weighing 185. Of course, we'd take a 250-pounder if he liked to pop somebody and could move."

Devaney said he came to Nebraska because he "believes people here are interested in football and have a proper attitude to help make a successful program."

During the 45-minute interview, Devaney dodged no questions.

Wyoming assistant coach Jim Ross, who accompanied Devaney Tuesday and who will move to Nebraska with him, will remain in Lincoln several days to talk with players on eligibility problems.

Ross served as end and defensive coach at Wyoming.

Devaney said John Melton, the head freshman coach at Wyoming, will also move to Lincoln and that other Cowboy staff members may also transfer.

Cletus Fischer and possibly one other assistant will be retained from the staff of Coach Bill Jennings, whose contract was not renewed.

Devaney said he will use the same multiple offense at Nebraska that he employed at Wyoming. The attack pattern was originated at Michigan State.

He said he likes the double-wing with split and slot backs and that he also uses the spread frequently along with the T.

Devaney, who lettered "37 to 39" at Wyoming last fall, uses alternate units.

Spring practice, Devaney said, will start in April and will be four days a week for five weeks.

Before spring practice, Devaney hopes to concentrate on recruiting, studying films to evaluate players and on encouraging players to stay in condition — and eligible.

At Wyoming, Devaney's squad had players from 18 states. Unless the university has some other policy, Devaney said, he will expect athletes on football scholarships to give football top priority.

He elaborated by saying he will expect sophomores on football scholarship to pass up spring sports on days on which there is football. The same will hold for juniors unless they are excused. When it was suggested previous Nebraska coaches had difficulty getting full attendance at football practice on certain days because of the conflict with classes. Devaney said:

"That is something I'll have to check. That could send me back to Wyoming mighty quick."

Devaney was only being facetious, however. He said he plans to move to Lincoln as soon as "I can get a house."

Asked if his son, Michael, a sophomore in engineering at Wyoming, would transfer to Nebraska, Devaney quipped, "If he's awarded a scholarship here, he'll probably transfer; otherwise he can't afford it."

Michael, although an all-state end in high school, is not a Wyoming footballer.

The Devaneys also have a daughter, Patricia, a high school senior.

Although Nebraska has come to terms with Devaney, the hiring was snagged temporarily Monday when Wyoming's Board of Trustees deferred action until a February 2 board meeting on his request for release from a five-year contract signed only last summer.

Devaney will leave today for the N.C.A.A. convention in Chicago where he will join N.U. Athletic Director Tippy Dye. After a visit to Ohio with Dye, he will probably meet Mrs. Devaney in Lincoln on his return west.

10

Devaney Release Uncertain

By THE ASSOCIATED PRESS
The Omaha World-Herald

LARAMIE, Wyo., January 10, 1962 — One of the trustees objecting to Wyoming Football Coach Bob Devaney's departure said Tuesday he was certain Devaney would get his release.

But the trustee, who asked not to be identified, added some of the trustees wanted to make Devaney sweat for a while.

Several trustees indicated they were disgruntled at having Wyoming's third coach in succession jump long-term contracts to move to larger schools. Bowden Wyatt and Phil Dickens each received releases before going on to new jobs — Wyatt to Arkansas and Dickens to Indiana.

11

N.U. Poised For Approval
Of Grid Pact

By UNITED PRESS INTERNATIONAL
The Omaha World-Herald

OMAHA, Neb., February 2, 1962 — The decks apparently are cleared for Bob Devaney to take the University of Nebraska football coaching duties.

The University of Wyoming Board of Trustees will meet today, presumably to release Devaney from the 4½ years on his Wyoming contract so he can accept the Husker post.

At Lincoln, the Nebraska Board of Regents has called a meeting for 5 P.M. today, apparently getting in position to act immediately on a contract with Devaney as soon as the Wyoming ties are broken officially.

While there has been some opposition among Wyoming trustees in giving Devaney his release, there appears little likelihood that they will hold the 46-year-old coach to his contract.

Wyoming Athletic Director Glenn Jacoby said he would recommend Devaney be given his release.

Cletus Fischer, a Nebraska assistant under the departed Bill Jennings, spiked rumors Thursday that he was interested in the Wyoming job.

"I've never applied for the Wyoming coaching job and don't intend to," Fischer declared.

He was commenting on a report of an unidentified fan who said he was boosting Fischer for the Wyoming position.

"I have accepted a job with Devaney at Nebraska," Fischer said. Wyoming Athletic Director Jacoby declined comment on the upcoming vacancy. He denied that the job already has been offered to Lloyd Eaton, the line coach under Devaney.

Jacoby said Eaton "has as good a chance as any but five or six others have an equal chance."

12

Wyoming Releases Devaney, Raps Dye

From WORLD-HERALD WIRE SERVICES
The Omaha World-Herald

LARAMIE, Wyo., February 3, 1962 — The University of Wyoming Board of Trustees let Football Coach Bob Devaney sweat until 10 P.M. Friday, then freed him to take a similar position at Nebraska.

The announcement, withheld for an hour after the trustees' meeting ended, was made on the public address system at the conclusion of the Wyoming-Utah basketball game in the university's fieldhouse.

It followed a meeting of trustees which lasted nearly six hours.

The board, which voted 8-4 to release Devaney, rebuked the coach and Nebraska Athletic Director Tippy Dye for the manner in which negotiations to hire Devaney were conducted.

An earlier vote had ended 7-5 in favor of releasing Devaney but it was decided another ballot should be taken.

The board statement said: "A coach should not enter into negotiations with a second institution during a term of a contract without first notifying the institution which is a party to his contractual agreement."

This apparently was a reference to Devaney's visiting the Nebraska campus while Wyoming Athletic Director Glenn (Red) Jacoby was vacationing in Idaho.

The trustees said they will take up the subject of appointing Devaney's successor today. Reports circulated that defensive coach Lloyd Eaton was in line to succeed him. Soft-spoken Devaney is following his two predecessors, Bowden Wyatt and Phil Dickens, in leaving a long-term Wyoming contract for the lure of a larger school.

Devaney is expected to take with him end coach Jim Ross, line coach Carl Selmer, freshman coach John Melton and backfield coach Mike Corgan.

He coached the Cowboys to all or part of the Skyline Football Conference championship in four of the last five years and piled up an impressive record of 35 victories, 10 losses and five ties.

The Cowboys under Devaney won the titles in 1958 and 1959 and tied with Utah State for the crown the last two years.

Wyatt, who transformed Wyoming from the Skyline Conference into a gridiron powerhouse right after World War II, had broken a long-term contract to go to Arkansas following the 1952 season.

Dickens, who coached the Cowboys for four seasons, moved to Indiana following an unbeaten season in 1956.

No Action at N.U.

No action concerning Football Coach Bob Devaney was taken Friday by the Nebraska Board of Regents. The board convened and adjourned without hearing from the Wyoming Board of Trustees at Laramie.

The regents previously authorized the hiring of Devaney, pending release from his Wyoming contract. Therefore, acceptance will be automatic.

Devaney's salary and the length of his contract may not be announced until the next formal meeting of the Nebraska regents.

13

Devaney Has Already Beaten Tough Opposition

By WALLY PROVOST
Special to The Omaha World-Herald

OMAHA, Neb., February 4, 1962 — Dr. K. F. Wirt of York, Neb., believes University of Nebraska football ticket buyers would be interested in the caliber of opposition involved in Coach Bob Devaney's record of 35 victories, 10 losses and five ties at Wyoming University.

That's a good point.

As the heartless gents at the cigar store might ask, "Who did he beat?"

Coast Scalp

In his five years at Wyoming, Devaney's teams dominated the Skyline Conference.

They won or shared the title each of the past four seasons.

Devaney was asked to state his most notable triumphs in non-conference play.

"In 1958," he replied, "It was the Oregon State game.

"Our team was made up mostly of sophomores. Oregon State was defending champion on the Coast, and had beaten U.C.L.A., the previous week.

"Wyoming won by 28-0."

Texans

In 1959, Devaney was proudest of his victory over North Carolina State, which, incidentally, will oppose the Huskers at Lincoln next October 13.

'The score was 26-0," Devaney remarked. "We played them at Raleigh, and it was homecoming."

The following year, Wyoming found itself facing unexpected trouble from Texas Tech.

"We had just lost to Utah State and we were beat up physically," Devaney recalled. "Texas Tech was fresh from a win over Tulane.

"The game was at Lubbock. We came from behind to win by 10-7. That probably was as satisfying as any victory during my stay at Wyoming."

K.U. Held

Two games of last season merit special attention.

Down, 14-0, Wyoming fought back for a 15-14 edge over North Carolina State, which had one of the year's outstanding quarterbacks in Roman Gabriel.

Quarterback Chuck Lamson, who had a great afternoon, provided the decisive extra point

"We were 13-point underdogs against Kansas but managed to get a 6-6 tie," Devaney continued.

"That was despite the fact Lamson was injured early and missed about three-fourths of the game."

Fischer

Fans will recall that during the recent period of coachless confusion at Nebraska, a large number of public and parochial school coaches in Omaha went on record as favoring Cletus Fischer for the top Husker post.

Although that unusual vote of confidence was commendable, it also created something of a delicate situation.

However, on his first full day and evening in Omaha after tentatively accepting the Husker offer, Coach Devaney met with those same Fischer boosters.

Who arranged that meeting? Omaha N Club president Bob Elliott says the credit must go to Fischer.

As the high school coaches had pointed out, Mr. Fischer is quite a man. Devaney says he is delighted to be working with him.

THE FIRST GAME

14

Cornhuskers Rout South Dakota

By GREGG McBRIDE
Special to The Omaha World-Herald

LINCOLN, Neb., September 22, 1962 — Nebraska lived up to Bob Devaney's promise of a full-throttle offense Saturday, beating woefully undermanned South Dakota University, 53-0, in the new coach's debut.

It was apparent to the crowd of 27,000 that Nebraska's fattest point production in 17 years was of no great significance.

But the rooters were delighted by the methods used in achieving victory.

The Cornhuskers came out shooting and completed 11 of 17 passes for 142 yards before mercifully holstering their biggest guns.

They introduced two new halfbacks with exciting speed — Dave Theisen and Kent McCloughan. They also exhibited three quarterbacks with aerial ability — Denny Claridge, John Faiman and Doug Tucker.

Defensively, they held South Dakota without a first down until midway in the third quarter — when the score had already mounted to 32-0.

But the victims were so completely overwhelmed — Nebraska used more backs than South Dakota had linemen in suit — that there was little indication of what can be expected in next week's test at Michigan.

Nebraska hadn't run up as many points since Potsy Clark's team of 1945 defeated the same school by the same score.

Saturday's rout started slowly enough. There was only a single touchdown in the opening quarter. It came on a 78-yard sweep originated by the first team and fulfilled by the No. 2 unit.

The payoff was a fourth-down play, with quarterback John Faiman pitching to Larry Tomlinson for 20 yards.

Tomlinson, a 6-foot-1 junior end, took the ball a couple of strides from the goal line and easily outmaneuvered defender Denny Hanson.

Faiman, who was used only four minutes last season, connected on three other passes for a total of 55 yards and two touchdowns.

The second score this day, however, was engineered by first-team quarterback Denny Claridge. Nine- and five-yard sprints by Rudy Johnson and a Claridge-to-Theisen pass for four yards helped set the stage for Claridge's long-striding gallop to the end zone from the 15.

This raised the count to a modest 12-0 midway in the second period.

A fumble by rookie Willie Paschall cost Nebraska possession on its next opportunity following a thrust to the South Dakota 3. Still in the second period, Theisen found McCloughan with a running pass for 14 yards. McCloughan raced wide to his left for 17 yards and fullback Joe McNulty romped over from the 2 for the third score.

When burly Jim Baffico, the former junior college all-America, kicked the conversion, Nebraska had its halftime advantage of 19-0.

The visitors had lost some of their stamina but none of their grit at this point.

On the second play of the second half, South Dakota quarterback Dick Walsh fired what appeared to be a sharp pass to fullback Ken Janvrin.

However, Theisen breezed into the picture at just the proper split second, leaped for the ball and came down running. The tall transfer student from Marquette kept kicking up his heels until he had covered the 27 yards required for a touchdown.

Just a couple of minutes later, Theisen gave another breathtaking demonstration of speed and maneuverability. He grabbed Hanson's punt on the Nebraska 43, skipped to the sideline as blocker Dick Callahan erased Mamon Keys and raced all the way to the South Dakota 27, where he was squeezed out-of-bounds by Walsh.

Husker halfback Willie Ross went over from the 15 on a sprint wide around right end three players. Nebraska was offside, however, shoving the ball back to the 20.

This time McCloughan, the sophomore from Broken Bow, Neb., fielded a lateral from Claridge and scooted all the way around the opposite flank. Several good line bucks by fullback Gene Young and a 7-yard keeper by Faiman put the ball on the South Dakota 14 with a couple of minutes remaining in the third quarter.

Under a heavy rush, Faiman fired a perfect pass to sophomore John Vujevich alone in the end zone.

Early in the fourth period, McNulty, the rookie from Wymore, Neb., contributed rushes of 8, 7 and 6 yards to a scoring drive of 54 yards. Paschall's offering was a 23-yard trip around left end.

With the goal line 2 yards away, Tucker got across on two straight keepers.

The first touchdown — with nine minutes to go — covered less than a yard and was the pleasure of veteran fullback Noel Martin.

It followed two outstanding pass plays — Tucker to end Curtis Bryan for 20 yards and Tucker to Martin for 14.

Although there was little opportunity to cheer the underdog, the crowd departed with great admiration for South Dakota halfback Dick Scott. The 5-foot-5, 151-pound junior from Watertown, Neb., produced 73 yards on 16 carries. One brilliant effort covered 25.

Scott was symbolic of a dogged but hopeless resistance.

*   *   *

In contrast to the confusion which has appeared to keep the Cornhusker bench in a turmoil during recent seasons, all was order and business-like on the Scarlet side of the field Saturday.

Players remained on the bench instead of roaming the sidelines.

Devaney gave the orders and his assistants carried them out.

The new coach spoke to the players as they left the field — a word of encouragement, advice or an occasional verbal whip.

Devaney, hoarse from a cold, could not do much shouting from the sidelines. Mike Corgan, an assistant coach, filled that gap.

Once it was obvious Devaney signaled from the bench. This was on a fourth-down-and-one-yard-to-go situation. The game was scoreless and the Huskers had possession on their 44.

"It probably wasn't a good call, but the quarterback (Claridge) looked over and I felt the boys could make it."

They did that, with fullback Warren Powers getting the first and 10 with a yard to spare.

The Nebraska bench got help from a Polaroid camera atop the press box.

Snapshots showing defensive alignment and spacing were peeled off and hurried to the field.

41

Devaney had mixed emotions about his inaugural.

The 53-0 score pleased him. His Cowboys had whipped Kansas State, 12-7, in his Wyoming debut.

Devaney also liked the work of his quarterbacks — Dennis Claridge, John Faiman and Doug Tucker. He thought Claridge ran and passed well. Faiman had his best afternoon (four for five) and Tucker, after an early attack of "sophomoritis," hit three for three.

The coach was disappointed the varsity "wasn't able to accomplish much until South Dakota tired."

Reviewing the game, he said, "We had pass receivers open early and our running attack bogged down the first half."

The showing after the intermission (34 points) left him feeling better. Devaney then swept the bench, emphasizing he had no intention of red-shirting any players.

During the 14-point last quarter, none of the first two units were used. The third string played six minutes and the fourth team the last nine. The third string also played much of the second quarter.

Devaney side-stepped singling out players for special praise, but he did give Dave Theisen a pat on the back for defensive play.

"We will have to do better at Michigan," he commented.

"And we'll have to get a lot tougher," Husker assistant coach Corgan added.

SCORE BY PERIODS

Nebraska 6	13	14	20	—	53
South Dakota 0	0	0	0	—	0

A JUST REWARD

15

Fans Present $200,000 Policy To Nebraska Football Coach

By UNITED PRESS INTERNATIONAL
The New York Times

LINCOLN, Neb., November 13, 1962 — Coach Bob Devaney, whose high-scoring Nebraska Cornhuskers have ended a long period of frustration for the state's football fans, today received an expensive inducement to stay with the Cornhuskers.

Devaney, who said he had "never considered leaving the university and never contemplated leaving in the near future," was presented a $200,000 life insurance policy paid for by Cornhusker boosters in a pointed effort to keep the popular coach.

At least two other Midwest football coaches also have received large life insurance policies. Dan Devine of Missouri was insured for $150,000 and Clay Stapleton of Iowa State for $100,000.

Despite rumors to the contrary, Devaney insisted he had received no offers since he came to Nebraska last January after a successful five-year stay at Wyoming.

The premiums on the fan-sponsored policy are $9,000 a year. Devaney draws $17,000 a year in salary, so, in effect, he received a pay increase to $26,000 a year.

Devaney, who is 47 years old, inherited a squad which won 3, lost 6 and tied 1 in 1961. He has put the Cornhuskers into national prominence by compiling a 7-1 record. Nebraska trounced Kansas, 40-16, last Saturday.

The insurance policy went into effect last Friday. Under its terms, it will be revoked if Devaney leaves the Nebraska job before 1968.

THE 1962
GOTHAM BOWL

16

N.U. Regents, Big 8 Okay Husker Bid In Gotham Bowl

From WORLD-HERALD WIRE SERVICES
The Omaha World-Herald

OMAHA, Neb., December 5, 1962 — Nebraska Athletic Director Tippy Dye said Tuesday night that the University's Board of Regents and the Big Eight Conference had approved the Cornhuskers' appearance in the Gotham Bowl December 15.

The Cornhuskers will meet heralded quarterback George Mira and his University of Miami (Fla.) Hurricane teammates in New York's Yankee Stadium.

Coach Bob Devaney's squad Tuesday needed only 10 seconds in a private meeting to cast a unanimous vote for acceptance of the bid.

Devaney, who said workouts would resume today, warned his players that one hundred percent effort in practice would be needed to prepare for their task.

Cornhusker team captain Dwain Carlson, a guard from Fullerton, Neb., said the team is anxious to redeem itself for a 34-0 shellacking it absorbed November 24 at Oklahoma.

Executive Director Robert Curran of the Gotham Bowl said in New York that the Cornhuskers were recommended by Missouri Athletic Director Don Faurot.

Curran said Nebraska was first contacted for the March of Dimes charity tilt last week and that a firm invitation had been extended Monday night.

"We won a major victory when Miami turned down the Gator Bowl to play in New York," Curran said, "and the Miami coach, Andy Gustafson, wants to play Nebraska."

The game will be nationally televised, Curran said, adding that the bowl has a two-year contract with the American Broadcasting Company.

Curran noted that if ABC doesn't pick up the option this morning the televising of the contest will be put up to the highest bidder.

Site for the 10 A.M. (Omaha time) game has been moved from the Polo Grounds, where last year only 15,123 watched Baylor topple Utah State, 24-9.

"Regardless of what may have been reported," a bowl spokesman said, "the only two invitations extended were to Miami on Saturday night and to Nebraska.

"This is the game we wanted and Miami wanted all along," he said.

Miami's losses in a 7-3 season were to Louisiana State (17-3), Alabama (36-3) and Northwestern (29-7).

The team whipped Pittsburgh (23-14), Texas Christian (21-20), Florida State (7-6), Maryland (28-24), Air Force (21-3), Kentucky (25-17) and Florida (17-15).

"We are happy to go," Devaney said in Lincoln. "The boys seem one hundred percent enthusiastic."

Devaney said the team will fly to New York City the morning of December 14 and return either the day after the game or on Monday.

Fifteen to 20 of the Cornhuskers tossed the football around at the practice field Tuesday afternoon in anticipation of the announcement.

Players have been keeping in trim by playing handball.

Devaney said practices will consist mainly of refresher drills. Squad condition is reportedly good.

Senior quarterback John Faiman of Omaha, who suffered a leg fracture prior to the Kansas game, is out of his cast but is not expected to be available.

17

Cornhuskers Begin Gotham Bowl Drills

From WORLD-HERALD NEWS STAFF
The Omaha World-Herald

OMAHA, Neb., December 6, 1962 — Gloves and parkas were in evidence Wednesday as Nebraska's football team opened drills for the Gotham Bowl game with Miami U. one week from Saturday in New York.

The temperature was 37 degrees and a 25-mile-an-hour wind whipped across the south practice field.

"I can't complain — it's better than rain or snow," remarked Coach Bob Devaney, whose sore throat was protected by a towel muffler.

He said 49 players will be in the party flying East the morning of December 14.

This includes quarterback John Faiman of Omaha, tackle John Strohmyer of Lexington, Neb. and guard John Dervin of Chicago, who have been injured and will not play.

One varsity player, tackle Monte Kiffin, will not make the trip. Devaney said the Lexington, Neb. junior is on university probation because of a student escapade the week following the Oklahoma game. Don Stevenson, the hulking junior center from Steelton, Pa., was at Kiffin's position Wednesday.

The Huskers promptly paid their respects to quarterback George Mira, Miami's record-breaking passer, by concentrating on pass defense.

Asked whether he rated Mira better than any aerialist Nebraska faced during the regular season, the coach replied:

"I hope he isn't any better than the one we went against at Oklahoma"

Devaney referred to Monte Deere, who hurled three touchdown passes in the Sooners' 34-6 victory.

The coach added:

"From what we have seen of the movies, Miami is strong at running as well as passing."

In the exchange with Miami Coach Andy Gustafson, Nebraska has films of the Hurricanes' victory over Kentucky (25-17) and Florida (17-15), and their 36-3 loss to Alabama.

Gustafson requested movies of Nebraska's triumph over Kansas and its defeats by Missouri and Oklahoma.

According to Devaney, the Huskers will do no scrimmaging. He said no practice session will run as long as two hours.

How close can Nebraska come to reaching top form in the time permitted?

"We'll be all right," he said. "We won't have any excuse about not being in shape. Kids this age can't get far out of condition in the short time since our last game."

He added that he does not anticipate any changes in the top two lineups, which carried most of the load at Oklahoma.

18

Gotham Bowl Tickets Go On Sale

From WORLD-HERALD NEWS STAFF
The Omaha World-Herald

OMAHA, Neb., December 6, 1962 — Tickets to the Gotham Bowl game at Yankee Stadium are expected to be placed on sale by noon today at the University of Nebraska ticket office in the Coliseum.

"A block of three hundred tickets was airmailed from New York Wednesday," Ticket Manager James Pittenger said. "I have no idea how many will be needed, but there is no limit on the number available."

The price is $5.50 per ticket.

Pittenger said Nebraska's section runs from the 40 to the goal line, adding: "The earlier the order, the better the seat."

Mail orders will be accepted. Checks must be made payable to the University of Nebraska.

Wives to Travel

The Huskers will be quartered at The Manhattan Hotel, at Fifth Avenue and Forty-sixth Street, in the Times Square district.

Wives of the players and coaches will be members of the official party.

Athletic Director Tippy Dye was in Kansas City for a Big Eight meeting Wednesday and hoped to learn whether the conference would finance a band trip to New York.

The cost has been estimated at $15,000.

Still No TV

Nebraska was reported receiving a guarantee of $50,000 from the bowl promoters, with the possibility of a percentage depending on total receipts.

As of Wednesday night, the Gotham Bowl lacked a television contract.

Nebraska must submit a budget for conference approval. Any profit beyond that sum would be shared equally by the eight schools.

Devaney on Run

Coach Bob Devaney continues to be the busiest member of the N.U. Athletic Department.

He was in Kansas City for a Big Eight coaches' meeting Tuesday. He supervised the first bowl workout Wednesday in Lincoln.

He will attend an alumni-sponsored dinner for the N.U. staff and high school coaches Thursday night in Omaha. Saturday night he is scheduled to speak at a football banquet in Pittsburgh.

The Devaney calendar calls for appearances in Grand Island on Monday, North Platte on Tuesday, Scottsbluff on Wednesday — and New York City next Friday and Saturday.

Package Deals

Allen Jones of the Omaha Junior Chamber of Commerce Wednesday announced a special Gotham Bowl package deal for Husker football fans.

The J.C.C. group will fly out of Omaha at 11 A.M. on December 14, arriving in New York City at 2:30 P.M. Rooms will be provided at The Waldorf-Astoria Hotel plus tickets to Broadway plays.

Tickets to the Gotham Bowl game between Nebraska and Miami will be provided between the 35- and 40-yard lines.

There'll be a free day in New York City Sunday up to plane departure time at 6:40 P.M. — with arrival in Omaha Sunday night at 8:30.

Cost will be $210 per person.

19

Devaney Bemoans Lack Of Bowl TV

From WORLD-HERALD NEWS STAFF
The Omaha World-Herald

OMAHA, Neb., December 7, 1962 — Nebraska is concerned over the likelihood its Gotham Bowl football game with Miami on December 15 will be viewed only by the customers at Yankee Stadium.

Coach Bob Devaney said Thursday it was his personal opinion "we would not have accepted the invitation had we known the game might not be televised."

Reached at the Big Eight meeting in Kansas City, N.U. Athletic Director Tippy Dye said he has not signed a contract for the New York appearance — but only because he has not been in his office for several days.

Devaney explained he had thought the game would receive nationwide TV coverage, making it possible for all Nebraskans and friends and relatives of the players to watch.

Asked whether failure to peddle the contest to a TV network might lead to cancellation, Devaney remarked:

"I can't say, but it might."

Director Dye said that eventuality was conceivable but improbable.

He added that ABC-TV apparently had declined to exercise its option to carry the game. According to Dye, bowl sponsors hope to interest other chains.

The Gotham Bowl game was scheduled for an 11 A.M. kickoff in New York to clear the decks for ABC's coverage of the Houston-New York pairing in the American Football League.

That meant the Huskers would have been aired at 10 A.M. in the Midlands, 9 A.M. in the Rockies and 8 A.M. on the Pacific Coast.

With the option untouched, however, Omaha's ABC-TV affiliate is planning to show a program called "Allakazam" at N.U. kickoff time.

According to Dye, the Gotham Bowl contract calls for Nebraska and Miami each to receive $50,000 or 37½ percent of the gross receipts, whichever is greater.

The percentage is in accordance with National Collegiate Athletic Association rules.

Devaney ordered an hour's drill in sub-freezing weather Thursday and "promised" further outdoor chores today.

The program again stressed pass defense.

Asked what defensive alignment he planned for the Hurricanes, Devaney smilingly replied that assistant Jim Ross had held out for a two-man line and nine-man secondary, "but finally compromised on a three-eight defense."

Miami quarterback George Mira looks so tough, Nebraska may request Canadian rules for the use of 12 men, Devaney added.

"Miami is a steady team defensively," the coach remarked. "No club has been able to do much against them except by passing.

"We will have to do considerable throwing."

Florida Popular

Nebraskans apparently are more interested in a winter respite in Florida than a sojourn in Manhattan.

Ticket Manager James Pittenger said Thursday afternoon his office had sold 46 tickets to the Oklahoma-Alabama game in the Orange Bowl.

He reported about 30 requests for Gotham Bowl reservations.

20

Gotham Bowl Head Sure TV Contract To Be Signed

From WORLD-HERALD NEWS STAFF
The Omaha World-Herald

OMAHA, Neb., December 8, 1962 — Contract negotiations for televising the Gotham Bowl Game next Saturday between Miami and Nebraska in New York have not been completed and probably will not be confirmed until next week, The Associated Press was told Friday.

The American Broadcasting Company has an option to renew its contract from last year when it televised nationally the game between Baylor and Utah State. However, a network spokesman in New York said that no commitment has been made, though he admitted that one has been under discussion.

The network said it does not expect a decision until next week.

Gotham Bowl promoter Bob Curran said the game will be televised, but admitted that he had not secured a national outlet. Curran said that if ABC does not take its option he will try and negotiate with an independent television production firm, Sports Network.

A CBS spokesman said his network was not interested in handling the game and NBC is televising the Liberty Bowl in Philadelphia the same day.

Earlier Friday, Curran, in New York City, assured University of Nebraska officials in Lincoln that the game will be televised.

John Bentley, the sports publicity director at Nebraska, quoted the promoter as saying in a telephone conversation, "I can assure you the game will be televised."

Nebraska Coach Bob Devaney indicated Thursday night the Huskers might pull out of the bowl game if it were not televised.

Husker Athletic Director Tippy Dye said Friday in Lincoln he had not yet received the game contract but added he was assured it was in the mail.

Devaney is at Pittsburgh for a weekend banquet appearance and a huddle with Pennsylvania high school stars. The prep talent has been lined up by freshman coach John Melton, who headed for Pittsburgh early in the week.

The Nebraska coach also will miss today's varsity drill.

With Devaney absent, assistants took over Friday.

The varsity worked on kickoffs and continued to hammer away at pass defense.

Assistant Mike Corgan revealed the Huskers will wear new red jerseys purchased for the game. They'll have long sleeves in case of cold weather.

The Cornhusker party will travel in two chartered planes and number at least 120, the Nebraska Athletic Department announced.

Travelers will include the 48 squad members and wives, coaches and administrative staff members and their wives and university brass.

It was announced that if the regents make the trip, it will be at their own expense.

Dye said Nebraska will tailor its traveling group to conform with the other Big Eight members (Oklahoma and Missouri) which have bowl assignments.

The Nebraska band will not make the junket. Dye said it would cost $20,000 to send the musicians, many of whom are scheduled to help present "The Messiah" on the campus the evening of the bowl game.

Dye said he understood the University of Miami band was making the trip under the sponsorship of the City of Miami.

The Cornhuskers' itinerary calls for three nights on Broadway with headquarters at The Manhattan Hotel.

21

Miami, Nebraska
Want Guarantee

By THE ASSOCIATED PRESS
The New York Times

NEW YORK, December 10, 1962 — The Gotham Bowl football teams, Miami and Nebraska, threatened today to pull out of Saturday's game here unless $50,000 was put into escrow to guarantee their expenses.

In response, the game's director, Robert Curran, predicted that the game would be played before a crowd of 30,000.

Curran declined comment, however, on the demands for an escrow deposit. He said:

"We always keep financial arrangements to ourselves. We let the schools make their own announcements. We're not a fly-by-night organization. We have a very good credit rating with the N.C.A.A.

"We have rented Yankee Stadium, we have hired the Hotel Astor's Grand Ballroom for the award dinner Saturday night and we have ordered 125 wristwatches."

Drew 15,000 Last Year

Last season, the Gotham Bowl game drew only 15,000 fans but paid the competing teams, Baylor and Utah State, a total of $100,000 within 32 days.

Except for that performance, Miami's athletic director, Jack Harding, said he wouldn't have kept his patience this long. Neither Miami nor Nebraska has received a contract so far.

Harding and William H. Dye, the athletic director of Nebraska, said their teams would require a minimum of $30,000 each for expenses. Dye said the Nebraska squad would not leave the campus until the money had been put up.

"The Board of Regents is very concerned about the money," he said.

Harding said he asked Curran a week ago for an expense guarantee but was told the money would have to come out of tickets and television rights.

The American Broadcasting Company, which televised the game last season, did not pick up its option this season. Curran then said he would try for a deal with Sports Network, Inc. Hay Sharp of Sports Network said his company was not planning to handle the game.

The National Broadcasting Company said it would not handle the game. Bill MacPhail, the sports director of Columbia Broadcasting System, said CBS probably would not be interested.

"We want to give Curran every chance," Harding said. "I think however, that we must have the money in escrow by Wednesday morning. We can't go into New York just on promises."

Harding said Curran had talked of guaranteeing the team $75,000 each, but he added, "I do not expect anything like that."

22

Gotham Bowl Chiefs
Talking Good Game

From WORLD-HERALD NEWS STAFF
The Omaha World-Herald

OMAHA, Neb., December 11, 1962 — Despite scare stories regarding financial guarantees, weather and publicity, most Gotham Bowl game principals were talking a good game Monday night.

"We have no thought of not playing," said Coach Bob Devaney, whose Nebraskans are scheduled to meet the University of Miami at Yankee Stadium on Saturday.

"I think the game will go on," said N.U. Athletic Director Tippy Dye.

Both Miami and Nebraska went ahead Monday with their plans on assurances that financial demands would be met and approximately $65,000 deposited in escrow by the bowl promoters to meet team expenses.

Athletic Director Jack Harding of Miami said he had been told that a check for "approximately $30,000 would be placed in escrow by Wednesday, according to our agreement."

Harding said arrangements had been made for the team to fly to New York on Thursday.

Dye said he is confident that the bowl will meet its financial commitments. He said bowl officials had assured by letter that the game would be televised, that a contract would be supplied and that the requested $35,000 guarantee would be placed in escrow, but the school has received "no evidence as yet."

Devaney yielded to winter weather and had his squad practicing indoors on Monday, the team's fifth workout since accepting the bid.

"You can say," quipped Devaney, "that from now on we're just planning on trying to keep warm."

The Nebraska coach said, "neither the boys nor the coaches are giving any thought to not playing. We're planning on playing Miami and trying to win a football game."

Speaking by telephone from New York, bowl promoter Bob Curran declared, "Our only trouble is that we suffer our growing pains in this great communications center where the whole world can watch.

"We'll have network television and we'll have the game."

Curran added:

"We didn't have TV (a television contract) a year ago tonight, but the game between Baylor and Utah State was carried by 194 network outlets."

The latest Gotham Bowl alarm was sounded Monday afternoon when Harding and Dye demanded that $65,000 be deposited to guarantee expenses.

Neither Nebraska nor Miami has received a contract.

Harding said he asked Curran a week ago for an expense guarantee but was told the money would have to come out of ticket sales and television rights.

Dye indicated Nebraska's squad would not leave the campus until the money was placed in escrow.

"This is my responsibility, and the Board of Regents is very concerned about the money," he said.

Regarding an advance deposit, Curran commented:

"We always keep financial arrangements to ourselves. We let the schools make their own announcements. This was discussed with the directors last week."

On the subject of the New York newspaper strike, the promoter said:

"The fans live in Long Island, New Jersey and Connecticut, and those papers are not on strike. We are working with them and we have tripled our radio and TV time."

The American Broadcasting Company (ABC) has not exercised its option to carry the Gotham Bowl game. NBC said it will not handle the game.

"We told them we would take a 24-hour look, but it's extremely doubtful," said sports director Bill MacPhail of CBS.

But Curran said he remained hopeful.

He also emphasized that full rental on Yankee Stadium has been paid, 125 wristwatches have been ordered, The Hotel Astor ballroom has been rented for an awards banquet and arrangements are being made for players to appear on the Johnny Carson TV show Friday night.

According to Curran, the long-range forecast calls for "clear and cold" weather in New York on Saturday.

"I'm confident we'll draw around 30,000, the largest college crowd of the year in New York," the promoter added.

Coach Devaney said space is a problem in fieldhouse workouts and that he might stagger workout times to give offensive and defensive specialists more elbow room.

Ticket Manager James Pittenger and athletic publicist John Bentley are to fly to New York today. The squad is scheduled to leave by plane Friday morning.

23

Husker Trip To Bowl Seems Assured; 'TV Contract Near'

By THE ASSOCIATED PRESS
The Omaha World-Herald

NEW YORK, December 12, 1962 — A promise to place $65,000 in escrow and prospects of a television contract combined Tuesday to all but assure the Gotham Bowl game on Saturday between Miami and Nebraska.

The post-season game took on a clouded atmosphere Monday when the two schools, concerned over the failure of bowl promoter Bob Curran to land a television tie-up, demanded expense money be placed in escrow before leaving their campuses for New York. Nebraska asked $35,000 expense money, Miami $30,000.

The beleaguered promoter averted the possibility of a cancellation by verbally guaranteeing payment of the expenses. The money is to be placed in escrow today.

Curran received a rude jolt when the American Broadcasting Company (ABC), which televised last year's inaugural Gotham Bowl game between Baylor and Utah State, decided not to pick up its option.

The promoter, however, said he has been negotiating with the Columbia Broadcasting System (CBS) and was hopeful an agreement would be reached soon.

"I've said all along the game will be televised," he said, "and it will.

"It's just a matter of price now, not a lack of interest. It's a matter of the amount of money we're being offered and how much we have been asking.

"I think we've got the best bowl game of them all," Curran claimed. "It's the only post-season game that's a toss-up and the fans here, despite the newspaper strike, are showing real interest. The

March of Dimes, which is handling the sales, tell me the advance ticket sales are good and we expect to draw around 30,000."

Curran said he was annoyed by the advance money requests on the part of Miami and Nebraska but added, "We will not let any financial thing stop the game.

"We're not a fly-by-night organization. We have a very good credit rating with the National Collegiate Athletic Association.

"We made certain of that when we paid off both teams last year within 32 days after the game. I expect no difficulty in meeting our commitments — and on time — this year."

Gotham promoters planned a game in 1960 but withdrew when they were unable to sign teams at the close of the college season. They got into business last season when they matched Baylor against Utah State.

The attendance was only 15,123, but the bowl managed to pay Baylor $65,000 and Utah State $35,000. That $100,000 was exactly the amount ABC paid for television rights.

Curran declined comment on a report from Miami that the N.C.A.A. special events committee had seriously considered dropping the Gotham Bowl from its approved list of post-season games but relented after a plea for "one more chance."

"The game will be played," he said. "I promise that."

24

Miami Agrees To Gotham Game; 'Nebraska Will Wait'

From WORLD-HERALD WIRE SERVICES
The Omaha World-Herald

OMAHA, Neb., December 13, 1962 — The troubled Gotham Bowl football game, the subject of hasty conferences all day and into the night, will be played on schedule at 10 A.M. (Omaha time) Saturday, officials said Wednesday night.

The matter of television, though, remained up in the air.

Confirmation that the game would be played came from University of Miami President Henry King Stanford. He had threatened to pull his team out of the scheduled game with Nebraska.

Dr. King said he had been informed that $30,000 would be placed in escrow to cover expenses for the trip. "The team plans to leave Thursday for New York on schedule," he declared.

In Lincoln, Nebraska Chancellor Clifford M. Hardin said he conferred with Dr. King regarding the expense money but had heard nothing from Gotham Bowl officials. Nebraska has requested $35,000.

Hardin said he assumed that if the bowl committee is putting the Miami funds into escrow "they will do the same for us. We will wait until Thursday morning to see if the deposit is made."

The Huskers do not plan to fly into New York until Friday morning.

A New York spokesman, who asked not to be identified, revealed that Miami was promised $75,000 and Nebraska $55,000 for the Saturday game.

Baylor drew $65,000 and Utah State $35,000 for last year's inaugural Gotham Bowl. Earlier Wednesday, Dr. King threatened to pull Miami out if expense money was not put into escrow. This prompted a hurried conference between Gotham Bowl officials and the office of Mayor Robert Wagner, the honorary chairman of the game.

Dr. King said the information that the funds would be put in escrow came through legal counsel for Mayor Wagner.

This immediately raised speculation that bowl officials had failed in their bid to get a national television contract.

Bob Curran, the executive director of the bowl, insisted that this was not the case.

"It's the same situation we had last year," he said. "You can look for it. We'll have it. I just can't say any more about it right now."

Curran confirmed that he had been in contact with Mayor Wagner's office but declined to give the source of the escrow funds.

"The game's on and we'll have television," Curran said. "It's been quite a day. You'll never know. I think we'll change the name to the 'Suspense Bowl.' "

A report that CBS had agreed to telecast the game provided the starting time was moved back two hours could not be confirmed.

However, such a possibility appeared squashed when the extra events committee of the N.C.A.A. ordered the 10 A.M. (Omaha time) start to avoid conflict with the telecast of the Liberty Bowl in Philadelphia. That contest will start at noon (Omaha time) Saturday.

Special Off

Plans for special cars on a train to carry Washington, D.C.-area Nebraskans to New York for the Gotham Bowl game Saturday between Nebraska and Miami have been cancelled.

About 50 Nebraskans in Washington have ordered tickets for the game, which would have been enough to fill the cars, *The World Herald* was told.

A majority of the Cornhusker rooters said they prefer to drive to New York.

25

'Money Deposited, Gotham Bowl Is On'

From WORLD-HERALD WIRE SERVICES
The Omaha Evening World-Herald

OMAHA, Neb., December 13, 1962 — As of early this afternoon, the Gotham Bowl football game in New York's Yankee Stadium Saturday morning is on — according to Gotham Bowl officials.

However, University of Nebraska Athletic Director Tippy Dye said in Lincoln that he "had not heard from the committee on the reported deposit of guarantee money."

The Associated Press had reported that "harried Gotham Bowl officials had deposited expense money for both Nebraska and Miami at the Bankers Trust Company in New York at noon."

Dye said he had received no confirmation, nor could he affirm The Associated Press report that "the television problem had been solved through a delayed presentation of the game for Saturday afternoon."

United Press International said a press conference has been called for "later this afternoon to discuss the television aspects."

Evidently, the last-ditch efforts of New York City Mayor Robert Wagner "saved the game."

After the Gotham Bowl officials had wrangled for 10 hours Wednesday, Wagner stepped in to guarantee the deposit of $30,000 in expense money for Miami and $35,000 for Nebraska.

The Associated Press said the 10 A.M. (Omaha time) start of the game still was in effect.

Two Omaha radio stations, WOW and KFAB and KFOR of Lincoln have been granted permission to broadcast the Gotham Bowl game from New York on Saturday.

Broadcast time is 9:45 for the 10 A.M. (Omaha time) game.

26

Decks Cleared For Nebraskans To Play In Saturday Bowl Tilt

From WORLD-HERALD WIRE SERVICES
The Omaha World-Herald

OMAHA, Neb., December 14, 1962 — Nebraska Athletic Director W. H. (Tippy) Dye indicated in Lincoln Thursday night that the stage has finally been set for the Cornhuskers' appearance Saturday in the Gotham Bowl.

Dye's clarification of Cornhusker intentions apparently cleared the final obstacle from presentation of the 10 A.M. (Omaha time) football contest in New York's Yankee Stadium.

Earlier, bowl promoter Robert Curran of New York had announced that $30,000 had been placed in escrow for the University of Miami and $35,000 for Nebraska.

Dye waited two hours after the Curran announcement, then reported, "We're planning on going."

He said the check for the Nebraska financial guarantee was given to N.U. Athletic Ticket Manager James Pittenger Thursday night and that certification of the funds for the check is to be made this morning."

"We won't leave until we find out, but we're going ahead with regular plans," he declared.

The Associated Press said it was reported that Pittenger served notice at 3:30 P.M. Thursday that Nebraska's $35,000 would have to be posted by 5 P.M. or the school would pull out. Nebraska's plans for a chartered flight to New York include departure from Lincoln's Municipal Airport at 8 o'clock this morning.

The traveling group includes players, coaches and university officials plus their wives. All will return to Lincoln on Monday afternoon.

In New York, meanwhile, the temperature was 21 degrees as Miami's team checked in.

"This is the same kind of weather we had last year when we played in the Liberty Bowl," Hurricane Coach Andy Gustafson noted.

Passer George Mira said he didn't think the weather would affect his passing.

"It might hurt the receivers some, but after they get warmed up a bit, it shouldn't present any problem," he added.

"The boys wanted to come to New York very badly," Gustafson said.

"I was sick last night when it looked like the game was going to be called off," said Ben Rizzo, a 205-pound senior who may sign a professional contract after the game.

"We were all worried," said fullback Nick Ryder. "Some of us called New York to find out whether the game would be played.

"You should have heard the cheering when we finally learned late at night that the game would be played."

Crowd of 35,000?

Gotham Bowl Ticket Manager Joe Gustafson said Thursday that advance sales indicate a paid gathering of 35,000.

"With the television deal and a crowd of 35,000, the promotion will pay for itself," said bowl promoter Robert Curran. "And everything we make above expenses will go to the March of Dimes."

Dennis Claridge was at the helm of the Cornhuskers' steamroller in 1962.

Nebraska fans await the team's arrival at the Lincoln Airport following the Cornhuskers' 36-34 victory over Miami in the 1962 Gotham Bowl.

Frank Solich (45) scampers for the Cornhuskers' second touchdown against Auburn in the 1964 Orange Bowl.

A stubborn Nebraska defense tries to halt an Auburn advance led by Tiger quarterback Jimmy Sidle (12).

Arkansas halfback Bobby Burnett (33) goes over the top hoping to penetrate a stingy Cornhusker front wall in the 1965 Cotton Bowl.

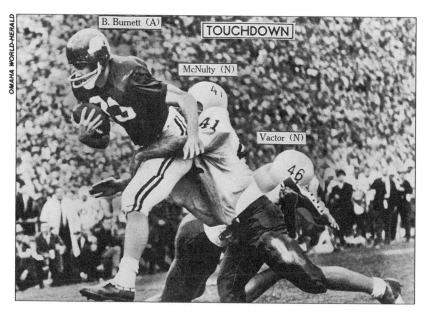

Nebraska defensive backs Joe McNulty (41) and Ted Vactor (46) spent much of the afternoon keeping Burnett from escaping for big yardage.

Solich (N)

Husker running back Frank Solich (45) attempts to elude a T.C.U. tackler in the 1965 season opener. Nebraska won this contest, 34-14.

15 YARD PASS

Jeter (N)

Lofquist (M)

Tony Jeter (84) was a clutch receiver for the Cornhuskers from 1963 to 1965. As a senior, he earned all-America honors.

Bob Devaney & Co. posted a 10-0 won-loss record during the 1965 regular season.

Against Paul (Bear) Bryant's Alabama Crimson Tide in the 1966 Orange Bowl, the Cornhusker juggernaut would finally meet an opponent who was just as tough. The Tide ended the evening with a 39-28 victory.

27

Husker Trip To New York Delayed During Gotham Cliffhanger

From WORLD-HERALD WIRE SERVICES
The Omaha Evening World-Herald

OMAHA, Neb., December 14, 1962 — It has to be an all-time record for sheer confusion — the cliffhanging prelude to Saturday's Gotham Bowl football game between Nebraska and Miami in New York's Yankee Stadium at 10 A.M. (Omaha time).

And Nebraska added a final touch to the proceedings this morning.

While the Husker team coaches and wives fretted at Lincoln's Municipal Airport in the post-dawn gloom, Husker Athletic Director Tippy Dye ordered a delay in the takeoff for New York.

"We won't leave until we are sure a check written by Gotham Bowl officials for $35,000 is good," Dye told the assembly.

The University had demanded the money be placed in a bank to assure team expenses.

Nebraska Ticket Manager Jim Pittenger in New York got the check Thursday night after the banks had closed.

Dye finally got the call he'd awaited; a message from Pittenger that the check had cleared — and the party took off, just two hours late.

There were whoops and hollers as players, coaches, university officials and wives got the word that the last hurdle to departure had been cleared.

Coach Bob Devaney burst out a door of the United Airlines operations room at Lincoln Airport and bellowed: "All right, we've been waiting a long time to get on these airplanes, now let's get on 'em."

A wild cheer went up as the travelers rushed for the planes.

Meanwhile the harried promoter of the bowl, Bob Curran, issued an optimistic statement from bowl headquarters:

"We'll draw 30,000 fans and they're going to see the most exciting football player in the country in Miami's George Mira," he told newsmen gathered for word on Nebraska's departure.

Curran's hopes for a break in the weather may be realized, with a forecast for temperatures in the mid-20's, but no snow.

That would be the only break, taking in account all the bungling and disorder that has gone on in preparations for the game.

Officials of both schools earlier threatened to pull their teams unless the $65,000 in expense money was put in escrow.

New York Mayor Robert Wagner got bowl promoters off the hook on that one by personally guaranteeing payment.

The confusion over television persisted right up to Thursday, when patchwork arrangements finally were made.

Meanwhile, Coach Andy Gustafson and his Miami players arrived Thursday afternoon amid guesses that Miami will receive $75,000 and Nebraska $55,000.

To which Curran replied:

"We never divulge financial terms, but those figures are not correct."

28

Dye Paces Till Check Is Cleared

From WORLD-HERALD NEWS STAFF
The Omaha Evening World-Herald

OMAHA, Neb., December 14, 1962 — Right up to the very end, the mass confusion enveloping Saturday's Gotham Bowl football game was setting new highs today.

As if the mad bungling and disorder during the week in New York wasn't enough, a final chapter was written at Lincoln's Municipal Airport in the post-dawn chill this morning.

With Miami already in New York City, the Husker party of players, coaches and wives assembled for an 8 A.M. take-off for New York.

Then came a hitch.

Nebraska Athletic Director Tippy Dye paced the airport corridors awaiting a telephone call from Nebraska Ticket Manager James Pittenger.

The ticket boss Thursday night had received a check for $35,000 guaranteeing Nebraska's expenses.

He got the check after the banks closed.

And Mr. Dye insisted there'd be no take-off until he heard from Mr. Pittenger that the check had cleared.

So . . .

While fretful passengers had second breakfasts and made last minute calls to remind Aunt Emma to turn off the oven, Mr. Dye paced.

And he paced. Finally, an hour and 45 minutes after scheduled departure time, the call came through.

"It's okay; the check cleared," Mr. Pittenger advised the relieved Mr. Dye.

There was a cheer from the gathering at Mr. Dye's announcement. And 10 minutes later the Huskers were winging to New York.

29

N.U.'s Long Suits: Balance On Offense, Depth In Line

By WALLY PROVOST
Special to The Omaha Evening World-Herald

NEW YORK, December 14, 1962 — The University of Miami doesn't claim everything for its all-America quarterback.

"George Mira is just short of a miracle," confesses publicist George Gallet on the eve of the Gotham Bowl football game with Nebraska at Yankee Stadium.

The Floridians arrived Thursday and checked in at The Hotel Barclay.

Nebraska's frosted footballers will pitch camp at The Manhattan Hotel, which also is bowl game headquarters.

Support for Miami is based on the club's 7-3 record against tougher opposition, the fact it was active a week later than the Huskers and the advantage of much better practice weather.

Andy Gustafson's Southerners still are preening over their upset of arch-rival Florida U. in the regular-season finale.

By contrast, Nebraska closed on a glum note — a 34-6 drubbing by Oklahoma.

However, it's not difficult to find backing for the Cornhuskers in the 10 A.M. (Omaha time) contest Saturday.

Nebraska is believed to be superior in offensive balance, ground power and line depth.

With quarterback Denny Claridge contributing 10 touchdowns, Nebraska outscored its opponents by a 257-127 margin during an 8-2 campaign. Miami fell short of its rivals' scoring, 155-181, but won all the close games.

Both schools can exhibit the type of beef New Yorkers are accustomed to seeing in the games of their professional Giants and Titans. Nebraska's jumbos such as Bob Brown (259), Jim Baffico (268) and

Lloyd Voss (245) are countered by Miami's Rex Benson (248), Bud Savini (245) and Joe Smerdel (235).

N.U. rooters believe Miami and Mira can be checked if the Huskers overpower the line. Gustafson has heard that song before.

"Mira never loses his poise . . . he has full control and command of the game at all times — so much so that we rarely ever send in a play," declares the coach.

"When pass protection for Mira breaks down completely, he's at his best."

The slim junior this season gained 323 yards rushing in addition to pass yardage of 1,732. But he was thrown for losses totaling 163 yards, and it's Nebraska's aim to fatten that figure.

30

Huskers Plan Early
Arrival At Stadium

By WALLY PROVOST
Special to The Omaha World-Herald

NEW YORK, December 15, 1962 — The ghostly Gotham Bowl becomes a reality today at 10 A.M. (Omaha time), when Nebraska's yawning Cornhuskers square off with Miami on the cold, hard turf of Yankee Stadium.

Fearing a frozen surface that will not yield to cleats, N.U. coach Bob Devaney has ordered an early arrival at the stadium for the purpose of testing tennis shoes.

To prepare for their scrap with the Floridians and their glamour-bathed quarterback, George Mira, the Huskers will eat breakfast at 6:30 A.M., receive a final briefing at 7 A.M. and depart by bus from their Manhattan Hotel headquarters around 9.

Because of the delay in securing firm assurance of the demanded $35,000 guarantee, the Huskers arrived more than two hours late Friday afternoon and were forced to skip a scheduled workout at the stadium.

In Devaney's opinion, "that won't make much difference."

In view of Mira's sensational passing record, reporters immediately questioned Devaney about Nebraska's aerial defense.

"At times it's been pretty good, and at times it's been pretty bad," the coach replied.

"Against teams that were supposed to be good at passing, our defense was pretty good."

He pointed out that Oklahoma, which used three touchdown passes in trouncing Nebraska in the latter's regular-season finale, generally had not put much emphasis on the overhead game.

Nebraska's job today is to check Mira, a junior who excels at the pass-run option, and to curtail the rushing of Nick Ryder, a native

New Yorker who hopes to impress the home folks.

Ryder's production of 607 ground yards is far the best total for either team.

In turn, Miami must alternately stave off and penetrate Nebraska's bulky lines — an achievement that no opponent made with any great degree of success this year.

On the attack, Nebraska for the first time this year has a completely healthy starting backfield of Denny Claridge, Willie Ross, Dennis Stuewe and Bill (Thunder) Thornton.

If Claridge's on-and-off passes are clicking and Thornton is in his best form, Miami's defenses will be thoroughly tested.

Devaney said he doubted that the near-comical confusion surrounding the Gotham Bowl the last 10 days had affected his squad adversely.

"We've worked all along on the assumption we'd play the game," the coach told newsmen.

"We've got a pretty good bunch of kids. They've been very cooperative. They wanted to make this trip and I'm sure they're happy to be here."

Asked whether Friday's flight delay rattled the players, halfback Ross guessed "not very much."

University officials would not permit the two team planes to leave Lincoln until Ticket Manager James Pittenger, in New York, personally saw that promised expense money was banked.

New York weather Friday was sunny but cold and windy. The forecast for today was "clear and warmer."

Because of the uproar surrounding bowl arrangements, and the handicap of New York's nine major daily newspapers being on strike, a small crowd is anticipated.

One bowl spokesman said he would be delighted if the turnout comes even close to the 15,000 for last year's Baylor-Utah State game.

31

Devaney: 'Huskers Won't Suffer Bowl Pitfalls Again'

By WALLY PROVOST
Special to The Omaha World-Herald

NEW YORK, December 15, 1962 — Bob Devaney let off pent-up steam on arrival here Friday, but he smiled as he talked and left a cluster of reporters roaring.

"I didn't think we'd ever see you in New York," a handshaking newsman said to the Nebraska football coach.

"Well," Devaney retorted, "I'll tell you right now, if I had it to do over, you wouldn't. That's for damned sure."

Not until the promoter's check for $35,000 was matched by money on deposit Friday morning did today's Nebraska-Miami Gotham Bowl football game progress beyond the talking stage.

There was a similar last-minute scramble for hard cash Thursday before the Miami squad departed for New York.

"We've been taking up a collection on the team, trying to raise enough to get the plane off the ground," Devaney told reporters.

Did Athletic Director (Tippy) Dye come?

"He's the guy who got us invited, and we haven't seen him since," Devaney remarked.

Governor Frank Morrison had urged acceptance of the bowl invitation on grounds that exposure in the "world's communications center" would be good for the school and the state.

New York's papers ceased publication because of a strike at about the same time Nebraska accepted.

Devaney's "audience" consisted of Nebraska newsmen, sports editor Tommy Devine of *The Miami News*, Robert Teague of *The New York Times* and an observer from Jersey City, N.J.

Teague said his interview would appear in West Coast and Paris editions of *The Times*, "exposure" not likely to bolster sagging ticket sales in New York City.

The New Jersey writer thought pleasantly in terms of the circulation his paper is "stealing" during the strike and, of Devaney, he declared:

"He's terrific. If they'd had a guy like this here Tuesday, they'd really have sold the game."

Incidentally, the expense money won't be placed in Nebraska's hands until Monday.

Because Nebraska must "perform" to fulfill its contract obligation and because banks are closed Sunday, Ticket Manager James Pittenger will pick up the certified expense-guarantee check at Banker's Trust on Monday morning.

Fourteen married players will do their sightseeing in company of their wives.

Following an awards luncheon in mid-afternoon today and a banquet tonight sponsored by the National March of Dimes Foundation, the Huskers will have "free time" until they assemble in the hotel lobby late Monday morning.

They are due to arrive in Lincoln at 2:45 P.M. on Monday.

32

Cornhuskers' Rally Tops Miami In Seesaw Thriller

By WALLY PROVOST and TOM ALLAN
Special to The Omaha Evening World-Herald

NEW YORK, December 15, 1962 — The postscript to the Nebraska football season will show that Bob Devaney's first-year coaching contributions included the school's first bowl triumph.

Devaney's Cornhusker inheritance included an 0-2 record in postseason competition — a 21-13 loss to Stanford in the 1941 Rose Bowl and a 34-7 thumping by Duke in the 1955 Orange Bowl.

"This will make them remember us as a bunch of fighters," the coach declared Saturday after his team had broken through the prestige barrier for a 36-34 triumph over Miami in one of the wildest offensive shows in bowl history.

This was the Gotham Bowl; a frantic, fledgling promotion that managed only 6,166 paid admissions in the midst of a newspaper strike and on a gray, 20-degree day. The number of spectators in the stands was less than one thousand.

Nevertheless, the victory will glow in the record books as a thriller in which Nebraska survived three Miami leads and two deadlocks to finally stab all-America quarterback George Mira with his own weapon.

Fittingly, it was Cornhusker quarterback Denny Claridge who stole a Mira pass to set up Nebraska's final touchdown and clinching point.

Equally appropriate, it again was Nebraska's defense which squeezed out Mira's dying gasp — a pass that the harassed Jack Sims could not hold and that guard Bob Brown snatched for the Huskers following a 49-yard thrust late in the final quarter.

In regard to the hair-raising finish — and the meager attendance — Nebraska assistant George Kelly spoke briefly and eloquently:

"The people of New York missed a helluva show today. They really blew it."

No one would belittle Mira the Matador, the hot-weather junior from Key West, Fla.

He smashed school records, with 24 completions and an amazing 321 aerial yards on the coldest day of his life. He shot the ball, he lobbed it and he threw it in beautiful high arcs.

Mira was voted the game's most valuable player.

But his circus performance and the 95 yards of bulling by Nick Ryder, a 205-pound New York native, were not sufficient to put down a plucky Husker gang that took the game on short notice and was handicapped by frigid practice weather.

There were plenty of headliners on the winners' squad:

— Claridge, the big, tough junior who passed for 146 yards, fed the ball expertly on handoffs, punted six times for a 37-yard average and played his unaccustomed defensive role to the hilt.

— Halfback Willie Ross, another junior, who raced 92 yards to a touchdown on a kickoff return and went 28 on a catch-and-run that kept a vital drive alive.

— Fullback Bill (Thunder) Thornton, whose swan song listed 4 yards of line-pounding, two touchdowns, a decisive conversion run and stout blocking.

— Halfback Dennis Steuwe, a senior whose rushing, kick returns and two pass catches were factors in Nebraska's repeated comebacks.

— End Dick Callahan, a red-headed junior who snagged four passes for 47 yards.

— End Mike Eger, a senior whose leaping catch of a 6-yard pass enabled the Scarlet to pull into a 20-20 deadlock shortly before half-time.

There was also tackle Lloyd Voss, who crashed into Miami's John Bennett to force the fumble that Dave Theisen recovered to set up Nebraska's first touchdown.

And young Kent McCloughan, who was pressing Sims when the Hurricane halfback failed to field the Mira pass that Brown picked off. Nebraska was overwhelmed in most of the statistics except the sweet numerical accounting that stands as the final score.

Mainly through Mira's dead-eye shooting, Miami out-first-downed Nebraska, 24-12. Ryder's heroics even enabled Miami to out-rush Nebraska, 181 yards to 150.

Meanwhile, the Huskers were playing tough, gradually putting more pressure on Mira and his receivers, gradually tightening their ground defenses.

Mira amassed more than two-thirds of his passing yardage (220) in the first half.

Losing Miami Coach Andy Gustafson paid tribute to Nebraska's offensive line play, keyed by guards Dwaine Carlson and Brown.

He observed that, "The Huskers were hitting our weak spots with the strength of their offensive attack. I kept switching tackles and ends on that side (Miami's left), but still we didn't stop them."

Gustafson admitted he was caught short on Husker kick-return tactics, stating:

"This was one of the new things that Nebraska did.

"In each of the films, they had consistently used a wedge on the kickoff returns and run up the middle. This time they caught us by surprise and went to the outside."

The Miami coach gave his subdued players a 60-second pep talk in the locker room following the game.

"Forget the loss," he advised, "and start thinking about our opener next September with Florida State."

Both coaches had the majority of their players in tennis shoes to obtain better footing on the frozen turf.

Regarding Mira's success, Devaney said: "We knew their pass patterns but we just couldn't stop them.

"The hard, slippery surface made it hard for the defensive backs to cut fast enough to adjust quickly to pass patterns.

"The field favored the receivers, who knew where they were going."

Assistant Gene Kelly told the Huskers:

"All right, boys. The Orange Bowl next year! The heck with this cold weather."

That was agreeable to everyone within hearing.

*   *   *

Perhaps not since the last time a Yankee opponent won a World Series here has there been such bedlam in the visitor's dressing room at Yankee Stadium.

That's where the Cornhuskers held the first chapter of their

Gotham Bowl victory celebration Saturday after defeating the University of Miami, 36-34.

By contrast, the stigma of defeat hung heavily in the locker room of the Miami Hurricanes, who used the Yankees' quarters.

Later in the afternoon the elated Huskers savored the spoils of victory at a Gotham Bowl luncheon. And Saturday evening at a March of Dimes banquet in the grand ballroom of The Hotel Astor on Times Square the Huskers accepted the huge silver Gotham Bowl trophy.

Then they were given free reign to enjoy themselves.

The victory will long linger in the memories of all, particularly the seniors.

They led the rush to hoist Coach Bob Devaney atop their shoulders. And it was to them Coach Devaney gave special handshakes for what he described as "one helluva ball game."

Bill Thornton said:

"This game evened it up for us seniors. We didn't like that ending at Oklahoma. Now we can feel good again."

With a big grin he added:

"Yes, and it was a good warm-up for those sophomores and juniors for next year's Orange Bowl."

Coach Devaney, whose geniality and quips have been a delight to the metropolitan press, had that old impish gleam in his eye as he received congratulations in the jammed dressing room.

The delays and frustration of sweating out the starting of this game were forgotten.

"No, this Gotham Bowl deserves a chance. Sure, they've got to get organized earlier and get things set up, but I think this ball game today will help their stock.

"If anything will save it, this game should.

"They (Gotham Bowl officials) didn't make any enemies."

Coach Devaney had "no comment" on the officials' call on an incomplete pass by George Mira late in the game. The Husker bench thought Mira was guilty of intentional grounding. He got rid of the ball — seemingly to no one — as Larry Tomlinson rode him to the ground.

"This was one of our best offensive games," Devaney said.

A New York scribe injected:

"Some people say Mira throws that ball too hard. What do you think?"

"Buddy, I'll accept him just the way he is," the coach answered.

Coach Devaney said he was glad the Miami quarterback "tossed just one too many."

That was the pass pirated by 250-pound Bob Brown.

"I ought to make big Bob a halfback," Devaney joshed.

The junior guard apparently has been infected by "Devaneyisms."

"It just felt great," he said of finding the deflected pass settle in his big mitts.

"Of course, I wanted to go all the way and I would have if I had just another good block or two and had. . . ." He lifted his size 13 feet in a mock sidestep.

"Yes," yelled Devaney, "and don't forget you also needed a good stiff arm."

SCORE BY PERIODS

Nebraska 6	14	8	8	—	36
Miami........................6	14	7	7	—	34

THE 1964
ORANGE BOWL

33

Nebraska Holds Off Auburn In Orange Bowl

By JIMMY BURNS
Special to The Miami Herald

MIAMI, January 1, 1964 — It was true what they said about Nebraska being a big, powerful and resourceful football team — worth its honors as Big Eight champion.

The Cornhuskers lived up to that reputation Wednesday as they stunned Auburn with 13 early points and then defended valiantly to score an upset in the 30th Orange Bowl Classic, 13-7, before 72,647 spectators and millions of television viewers. The Tigers of the Southeastern Conference had been favored by a point.

Quarterback Dennis Claridge staggered Auburn with an Orange Bowl-record 68-yard touchdown dash on the second play after Nebraska received the opening kickoff. Claridge's excursion around right end was a yard longer than the run Ned Peters (Ole Miss) made against Catholic U., here in 1936.

Dave Theisen added record field goals of 31 and 36 yards in the first and second quarters. The longest previous field goal was a 22-yarder by Bowden Wyatt (Tenn.) against Oklahoma in 1939.

In 16 minutes and 55 seconds, the rampaging Cornhuskers had grabbed a commanding lead and rattled the Tigers. The two teams quit for the intermission with no more scoring and the prospect of the game becoming a rout.

The badly-rattled Tigers regained some of their poise in the second quarter and quickly injected suspense after regrouping their forces at halftime.

Auburn quarterback Jimmy Sidle moved his team 71 yards in seven plays to score a touchdown with three minutes and 32 seconds remaining in the third period.

This made it a new game and the Tigers had the fans on their feet roaring as they launched one final drive from their 20-yard line in the last seven minutes. They were stopped short of a tying touchdown at Nebraska's 11.

It was the most competitive of the last three Orange Bowl games and the pre-game and halftime extravaganzas produced by Ernie Seiler delighted the crowd. In 1962, Louisiana State battered Colorado, 25-7, and last year Alabama shut out Oklahoma, 17-0.

Coach Bob Devaney had told his Cornhuskers that the prestige of their Big Eight was at stake, and his players responded. It was the first time in four tries that a Big Eight team had beaten a Southeastern Conference opponent in this classic.

The surprising feature was the Cornhuskers matching the Tigers in speed and topping them in punting and field goal kicking. Claridge directed his team well and ran for 108 yards, 12 more than Auburn's Sidle, who also was noted for his skill in working option plays.

Nebraska also lived up to its reputation as the nation's No. 1 rushing team, gaining 220 yards on the ground. But the Tigers played to their defensive rating (seventh in the nation) by limiting the Cornhuskers to that one quick touchdown.

Sidle completed 12 of 25 passes for 141 yards which gave Auburn the advantage in rushing and passing of 283 to 234 yards. This was scant consolation, particularly for the 14,000 Auburn fans who had no inspiration to scream their battle cry of War Eagle until the second half.

The Tigers had trouble handling Nebraska's all-America guard Bob Brown early, but he tired. The standout for the Cornhuskers was Tony Jeter, the 19-year-old right end who frustrated the Tigers time and again. Auburn's Howard Simpson, the left end, was the more valiant of the Tiger defenders.

Auburn's offense suffered when Tucker Frederickson suffered cracked ribs and was forced out of the game. His blocking had been a help, but early the Tigers had trouble handling those big Cornhuskers.

The Tigers made their first mistake after winning the pre-game toss. They elected to kick off. Coach Ralph (Shug) Jordan explained that they wanted to take advantage of wind, which was 13 m.p.h. out of the northwest. At kickoff time, the temperature was 68 degrees under hazy skies. The humidity was at 49 percent, but it must have seemed like 100 to the startled Auburn supporters moments later.

Frank Fuller kicked off and Kent McCloughan, catching the ball at his 8, whizzed back to Nebraska's 26 where he was dumped by Frederickson. The Tigers' poor defense on kicks hurt them throughout the game.

The Cornhuskers telescoped the Tiger line and Rudy Johnson found right tackle good for 6 yards before Bill Cody tackled.

There was no cause for alarm until Claridge kept the ball and made the most electrifying play of the game. He swung towards the northern boundary as Cornhuskers dumped Tiger defenders. Claridge stuck close to the sideline, outrunning all pursuers. Billy Edge got close enough to miss a tackle at Auburn's 22.

Fred Duda held the ball and Theisen kicked accurately to put Nebraska ahead, 7-0. The fans settled back in anticipation of Auburn rebounding.

George Rose ran Larry Tomlinson's kickoff back 18 yards to his 29, but the Tigers could not make a first down, Sidle being tossed for a 3-yard loss by Jeter.

Frank Solich returned Kilgore's punt to Nebraska's 42 — another lapse by the Tigers. The Cornhuskers then drove to Auburn's 11, where the Tiger defense stiffened. With Duda again holding, Theisen kicked the 31-yard field goal. Nebraska had 10 points in less than as many minutes.

A break gave Nebraska its third and final scoring chance. Rose fumbled Claridge's punt at his 25 on the first play of the second quarter. Jeter recovered for Nebraska at Auburn's 22. The Tigers yielded only 3 yards on as many tries and Duda and Theisen teamed perfectly again, making good the 36-yard kick.

The Tigers appeared confused and illegal procedures cost them chances to penetrate Cornhusker territory.

Auburn came back more determined and after an exchange of punts in the third quarter, got a drive going from its 29. Sidle fused it with a 28-yard pass to Bucky Waid.

Sidle was running more effectively and registered two first downs in a row — the last one a 13-yard excursion around right end. Mickey Sutton rammed left guard to reach Nebraska's 13.

Sidle dropped back in the shotgun formation with the Tigers' strength shifted to the left. He then followed his blocking around left end to score. Woody Woodall kicked the extra point and Auburn was behind only 13-7, with three minutes and 32 seconds left in the third quarter.

An exchange of punts started the Tigers from their 20 when Claridge punted into the end zone. There was still time for the Tigers to win with seven minutes and 32 seconds remaining.

Sidle completed five passes in the final sortie, the most effective being for 18 yards to Rose to put Auburn at Nebraska's 17. Rose caught a pass to reach the 11, but Bruce Smith broke up a fourth down toss intended for Doc Griffith and Nebraska took the ball and the game.

SCORE BY PERIODS

Nebraska 10	3	0	0	—	13
Auburn 0	0	7	0	—	7

34

2-Yard Play Breaks Up Game By Becoming A Long Touchdown

By UNITED PRESS INTERNATIONAL
The New York Times

MIAMI, January 1, 1964 — Nebraska credited a "two-yard play" today for its 13-7 triumph over favored Auburn in the Orange Bowl football game. The play was turned into a 68-yard touchdown.

"It surprised me as much as it surprised Auburn," said the Nebraska quarterback, Dennis Claridge, who ran for the 68 yards on the second play from scrimmage.

Claridge's touchdown, after only a minute 13 seconds of play, rattled Auburn so badly that the Southeastern Conference team fumbled and misplayed throughout the first half.

The Nebraska coach, Bob Devaney, said his Big Eight champions "had a real close shave." His players praised Auburn as "the hardest playing team we ever went up against."

"They sure came on like gangbusters in the second half," said Claridge. The big quarterback called the play on which he made his long run. He said it was a "quarterback trap good only for one or two yards a couple of times a game."

Claridge, who is trying to decide whether to play professional football for Green Bay or continue his plans for becoming a dentist, said his rival quarterback, Jimmy Sidle of Auburn, was "simply great."

"We had to shift defenses constantly in that second half," Devaney said. Nebraska stopped an Auburn drive for a score on the 11-yard line with 1:30 left to play.

In the Auburn dressing room, Sidle threw down his helmet in a show of dejection for having missed making a first down on

Auburn's last drive. Coach Ralph Jordan said Sidle did right in passing on the option on the final play. "We didn't think he could take it across running," Jordan said.

"We got after people in the second half," Jordan said. "I told 'em that's what they would have to do if they didn't want to go home embarrassed. They just got started too late after being hit by a little old 2-yard gainer that broke up the whole ball game."

THE 1965
COTTON BOWL

35

Hogs Overtake Nebraska In Cotton Bowl In Storybook Style

By WALTER ROBERTSON
Special to The Dallas Morning News

DALLAS, January 1, 1965 — Unmistakably, Cinderella is a fraud.

Arkansas' Razorbacks proved it with an incredible flare on an unsettled and unsettling New Year's Day Friday to claim a stirring 10-7 Cotton Bowl victory over Nebraska.

For Nebraska had already turned the storybook 1964 Razorbacks into pumpkins when Arkansas quarterback Freddy Marshall, shorn of his magical slippers for more than three quarters by a clearly dominant Nebraska team, suddenly updated the old fairy tale to drive the Razorbacks on an 80-yard touchdown drive that spelled victory less than five minutes before midnight.

It was a fitting finish to a blissful, unbeaten season for Coach Frank Broyles' Razorbacks — a team that gathered momentum each week like perhaps no other team in Southwest Conference history.

It was the more blissful because it gave Arkansas its first Cotton Bowl victory ever as a Southwest Conference host team, and because it gave Broyles a bowl victory after three straight defeats in 1961, '62 and '63.

Before Marshall — a study in confidence when all about him seems chaotic — set the Razorback sights on the Cornhusker goal line 80 long yards away with just nine minutes to play, few among the usual packed Cotton Bowl audience would have predicted it would come to pass.

After Arkansas had grabbed a 3-0 lead on Tom McKnelly's seventh field goal of the season, from the 21-yard line, Nebraska had controlled the game. The Huskers took the lead with 7:45 to play in the second quarter on a 69-yard drive spurred by a 36-yard pass from quarterback Bob Churchich to sophomore speedster Harry Wilson.

They had maintained it rather easily through the next 30 minutes of play as a defense headed by end Langston Coleman, nose guard Walter Barnes and tackles John Strohmeyer and Dick Czap seemed to shatter the usual Arkansas confidence, especially in its running game.

Marshall, whose uncanny ability on the sprintout options and slashing cutbacks at the tackles had geared the Razorback offense all season, couldn't get the team moving as it appeared the tongue-in-cheek warning they might throw 25-30 passes might be carried out.

Only once after the Arkansas field goal had the Razorbacks managed to put as many as two first downs together. And the only time they crossed midfield after the field goal, a clipping penalty shoved them back from the Nebraska 44 to their own 37 to scuttle that bit of cheer for Porker fans.

The Arkansas defensive unit — which later yielded its first points in six games — had been called upon to repel a Husker thrust that owned a first down on the Arkansas 15-yard line late in the first quarter. And a Nebraska field goal attempt from the 37 late in the third quarter was short. Otherwise the task Marshall faced as he broke his team from the huddle for that last desperate effort would surely have been impossible.

But on first down from the 20, following a Nebraska punt into the end zone, Marshall passed finally with the authority he has known all season. He hit end Jerry Lamb for 12 yards. Then a swing pass to the left flat to reserve tailback Bobby Burnett, the late-season sensation for the Razorbacks, moved for 11 yards and a first down at the 43. Two plays later Marshall connected with wingback Jim Lindsey for 10 yards and a first down at the Nebraska 43.

Then Marshall displayed the running ability which had been such a factor in the Razorbacks' great season but such an insignificant one previously in this game. He ducked up the middle as the Huskers rushed with fury, somehow disentangled himself from a mass of humanity near the line of scrimmage and exploded into the secondary with his short legs clawing and churning frantically. He netted 10 yards for a first down at the Nebraska 33, although he picked up a badly-cut mouth as he battered his way through the wall of defenders.

But he nevertheless swung back toward the fierce conflict between two superb and determined lines on the next play. As he stepped into turmoil, surely no more than a yard behind the line of scrimmage at left tackle, he shot a right arm above the fury and rifled the ball in the direction of Lindsey who had maneuvered to the left sideline and suddenly cut straight down it at full speed.

Lindsey took the ball with a lunge at the 20-yard line, played a momentary game of zig and zag with a couple of Huskers trying desperately to get a shot at this streaking missile. They didn't before Lindsey had stabbed to the 4-yard line.

From there Marshall turned things over to Burnett, the junior from Smackover, Ark., who had played such a big role in the Porkers' last two regular-season victories.

Burnett got only one yard on his first try. But he took a wobbly pitchout from Marshall on second down as he thundered toward the right flank, left his feet with a great burst of determination as he was challenged at the line of scrimmage and exploded through two defenders for what had to be one of the most satisfying touchdowns in Arkansas history.

There was just four minutes 41 seconds to play when the Razorbacks finally scored. And it was only left for Jim Williams, one of the Razorbacks' pair of magnificent defensive tackles, to storm through to blast Churchich for a 15-yard loss as he tried to pass on fourth down and seal an incredible win for Arkansas and a sickening loss for the underdog Huskers.

There was still a minute and 20 seconds to play when Williams picked himself up off Churchich's flattened frame, but Loyd Phillips, the great sophomore running mate of Williams, picked up his fellow tackle and whirled him about in an uncontrolled if premature celebration.

Williams, Phillips, all-America linebacker Ronnie Caveness, who was voted the game's outstanding lineman, and their fellow stalwarts of the touted Arkansas defense, generally had another fine afternoon, despite allowing the touchdown which was the first scored against the Porkers in more than 325 minutes of playing time, or since Texas' final touchdown in Arkansas' 14-13 victory which lit the fuse for a glorious season.

But for much of the afternoon it appeared a couple of big plays by Wilson, the splendid Husker soph, who Nebraska fans have dubbed "Lighthorse Harry," would obliterate all the Porker defensive heroics.

It was Wilson's grab of the 36-yard pass from Churchich early in the second period which led to the Husker touchdown. He raced away from Porker end Jim Finch down the right sidelines after the Nebraska ends had lured away deep Arkansas defenders Billy Gray and Harry Jones.

He took the ball inches away from the right boundary line and danced along it before Finch finally tripped him up from behind at the Arkansas 19.

Then from the 11, Wilson ripped behind left guard to the 1 and carried over on the next play with 7:45 left in the second period.

And as Nebraska fought to cling to that 7-3 lead against a stout south wind in the final period, it was Wilson who appeared to have put the Huskers out of danger. He flashed into the clear past Jones on a left end sweep and cruised 45 yards before Gray finally outmaneuvered an official to get to him at the Arkansas 35.

The inflamed Razorback defense stalled the threat at the 31 but there had been little to make one suspect the Porkers ever would be able to fight back from so deep in their own end of the field.

But Marshall, voted the game's outstanding back by a substantial margin over Wilson, waved his magic wand and the Arkansas offense emerged from its pumpkin shell.

SCORE BY PERIODS

Arkansas	3	0	0	7 —	10
Nebraska	0	7	0	0 —	7

36

The Sadness and Gladness

By SAM BLAIR
Special to The Dallas Morning News

DALLAS, January 1, 1965 — Late in the third quarter you could look at the rival head coaches on the sidelines and know who was winning the game. Bob Devaney stood calmly among his Nebraska troops a cool, calculating commander in a navy blue sports coat and a snappy tyrolean hat. But across the way Frank Broyles was enduring untold torture as his retreating Arkansas defense dug in on its 30-yard line. He was coatless, his shirt-tail was out, and he was nervously pacing a yard or so inside the playing field.

Eventually all his suffering proved worthwhile. However, somehow Broyles' Razorbacks kept their tormentors from improving on their 7-3 lead and a little later they did it again. Then . . . Wham, Bam! Alacazam! The Arkansas offense stormed back from wherever it had been hiding and ambushed the Cornhuskers with that beautiful 80-yard touchdown drive. The sideline scenes changed abruptly.

Broyles still was no fashion-plate, but his sweat-soaked shirt and dusty slacks took on new dignity as he watched the Arkansas defense deny Nebraska's last bid. His face, lined with tenseness and anxiety most of the afternoon, relaxed. All around him red-jerseyed players jumped and screamed and thrust one finger into the air, conducting their own impromptu national football poll as a fading clock put the finishing touch to a 10-7 victory.

Devaney didn't seem so cool now. He looked a little peeved and you really couldn't blame him. His team had been superior most of the afternoon, yet there was nothing left to do but accept defeat and trudge to the locker room.

He met Broyles in midfield for some brief pleasantries, then turned away. A photographer yelled, trying to summon Devaney back for a picture with Broyles but he wasn't having any. He waved the fellow off with both hands, sort of a "phooey-on-that-stuff" gesture.

No Place for Whispers

That certainly was Devaney's privilege. He had a right to be deeply disappointed, just as Arkansas had a right to be extremely proud. It was that kind of game.

Both sides did what they knew how to do best. Arkansas' execution simply was more timely. The Southwest Conference champions saved their best for last or, more accurately, they produced their best when anything less would have been worthless. That's what champions are supposed to do.

As the Arkansas players streamed into their locker room, bloody-mouthed heroes like Jim Lindsey and Fred Marshall dabbed happily at their wounds and the Razorback band made enough racket to make you glad they don't play these New Year's Day games at 3 A.M. If anyone's head was throbbing, however, it was forgotten inside the locker room.

Broyles, almost a basket case 30 minutes earlier, was the most expansive man in the Cotton Bowl now. As he raved on and on about the tremendous character of Arkansas' finest team ever and the worthiness of his opponent, an assistant interrupted him.

"Loyd Phillips (the raging sophomore defensive tackle) wants to know if it's all right with you if he rides back to the motel with his brother."

"Yeah . . . sure!" Frank enthused. "I'll carry that boy back on my shoulders if he wants me to."

Cause That Refreshes

It was defenders like Phillips, fellow tackle Jim Williams, linebacker Ronnie Caveness and halfback Ken Hatfield who had kept the Hogs within reach of victory when the offense seemed unable to do anything more impressive than jump offsides. Lindsey, Marshall, Bobby Burnett, Jerry Lamb & Co. earned their tributes in that final game-breaking drive but they weren't forgetting why it was possible for them to become heroes after all of their setbacks.

Lindsey had the game ball stuck securely in the top of the locker but he had no intention of keeping it:

"It's just there for safe-keeping," the rangy wingback explained. "We're going to give it to Hatfield, I think,"

And what had Broyles told his team at halftime? The coach admitted his words didn't remind anyone of Knute Rockne.

"I just said, 'Let's get better.' That's about all I could say.

"All of us knew that a team like this one, with a perfect record and all of its honors, has plenty of pride and determination. We just waited and hoped and in the fourth quarter, they proved how much they wanted this game."

You heard that and you remembered what you had seen and you felt glad for Arkansas. Then you remembered Devaney starting his lonely walk to the locker room and how strong his team had looked at times and you felt sad for Nebraska. It was just that kind of game.

THE DEVANEY
MAGIC

37

Bob Devaney:
Organization Man

Newsweek

OMAHA, Neb., October 4, 1965 — Pudgy Bob Devaney doesn't match the current image of the new breed of college football coach. Unlike suave young Ara Parseghian, John McKay and Darrell Royal, the 50-year-old Nebraska head coach resembles Wallace Beery rather than Kirk Douglas.

But the 5-foot-10, 200-pound Devaney has magic qualities that alumni like. Devaney, says Michigan State Coach Duffy Daugherty, who recommended him for the present job, "is like an old shoe — you want to turn back to him after those stylish, narrow new ones start pinching your feet." And there is a more important plus — his teams win.

Devaney, who spent fourteen years coaching high-school teams in Michigan, is the winningest college coach in the country. His three Nebraska and five Wyoming teams have given him 63 victories, fifteen losses and five ties.

For Nebraskans, it has been a pleasant change. Under Devaney the school has had as many winning seasons as it had in the preceding 21 years. The football boom is being felt all over town. Lincoln's board of education will open its first evening class next week for housewives who want to learn the difference between split pea and the split T.

Devaney's theory for producing winning teams is simple: "Recruit like hell, then organize." Only the work is hard. He and his staff make the usual talent searches in such well-known football factories as Steubenville, Ohio, and Uniontown, Pa. Only 31 of his 81 varsity players are state-bred. Devaney doesn't mind: "Nebraskans want to win more than they want to field an all-Nebraska team." But he doesn't neglect the local crop; last spring's cultivation has produced 22 state high-school stars.

A marvelous analyst of talent, Devaney gambles that an unlikely player will develop. This year's star back is Frank Solich, a 157-pound fullback from Cleveland, Ohio, who had to put 5 pounds of lead in his pants at the annual weigh-in so his weight would be more impressive in the game programs.

Once on campus, talent is carefully organized by Devaney and his assistants, a group of successful high-school coaches rather than ex-college stars. They even hold 8:30 Sunday morning workouts.

This year, the system is paying extra dividends. The Associated Press pre-season poll named the Cornhuskers to win the national title. After trouncing Texas Christian, 34-14, on opening day, they whipped Air Force, 27-17, last Saturday as Solich scored on runs of 80, 21 and 41 yards.

Meanwhile, Nebraska keeps its coach happy, too. It pays him a $22,000 salary (the university chancellor, Dr. Clifford Hardin, earns $29,500). Devaney earns another $25,000 making speeches and appearances. Boosters have bought him a $200,000 life-insurance policy, and he is supplied with two courtesy cars by local Pontiac and Dodge agencies.

The fanfare and fans' gifts have impressed Devaney, who bounced around to such stops as Big Beaver, Keego Harbor and Alpena high schools after graduation from little Alma College in Michigan. He no longer bothers to keep the family trunk packed.

38

Devaney —
Rhymes With Uncanny

Time

OMAHA, Neb., November 19, 1965 — Outside of maple leaves and football, the best thing about autumn is that you don't have to worry about hay fever any more. Especially if you live in Nebraska, where the goldenrod is the state flower. There aren't many maples in Nebraska, and there wasn't much big-time football — give or take a season or so — until a paunchy, puffy-eyed Irishman named Bob Devaney took over as head coach at the University of Nebraska in 1962.

Only twice in their history had the Cornhuskers been ranked among the nation's top ten. They had not won a Big Eight championship in 21 years. They had been invited just twice (in 1941 and 1955) to post-season bowl games, and lost both times. Their most beloved player, halfback Lloyd (Wild Hoss of the Plains) Cardwell, never made anyone's all-America in the 1930's. The coaches were mostly men who went on to become famous at some other school, like Fielding (Hurry-Up) Yost and Dana X. Bible.

But Devaney, as every Nebraskan knows, rhymes with uncanny. Bob walked out on a new five-year contract at Wyoming to take the Nebraska job, and announced on his arrival in Lincoln: "I don't expect to win enough games to be put on N.C.A.A. probation. I just want to win enough to warrant an investigation." Devaney proceeded to win 28 out of his first 33 — and improve from there. Until last week the closest the Cornhuskers had come to losing this fall was a 16-14 victory over No. 8-ranked Missouri. They won comfortably against Texas Christian (34-14), Air Force (27-17), Colorado (38-13) and Kansas (42-6); against Iowa State, Wisconsin and Kansas State, they ran up a combined score of 122 to 0. But last week the No. 3-ranked Cornhuskers ran into a hornet's nest at Stillwater, Okla., and almost got stung. Trailing, 17-14, in the last quarter, they marched 74 yards in 15 plays to take the lead, 21-17, with only 38 seconds left. But Oklahoma State wasn't quite through yet. It took a desperate tackle on the 5-yard line to make that score final and sew up the Big Eight championship for the unbeaten Cornhuskers, along with a trip to the Orange Bowl on Jan. 1 — their fourth bowl trip in as many seasons.

One Day at the Organ

If N.C.A.A. gumshoes are dogging Devaney's footsteps, he is leading them on a merry chase. He is the most peripatetic recruiter in Nebraska's history. No fewer than 68 of the 109 athletes who tried out for the team last spring were non-Nebraskans. The Huskers do have Nebraskan Bob Churchich playing quarterback, but he has to alternate with Chicago's Fred Duda. Another Chicagoan, 240-lb. tackle Walt Barnes, is the bulwark of a defense that so far has limited its opponents to 195 yards per game. Cleveland's Frank Solich may be the smallest fullback (at 5 feet 8 inches and 158 lbs.) in major college football, but he has gained an average of 5.5 yards per carry. Split end Freeman White, a 6-ft. 5-in. 220-pounder and All-Big Eight in 1964, comes from Detroit.

Then there is right end Tony Jeter. Jeter hails from Weirton, W. Va., and he was set to go to Arizona State before Devaney dropped by — just as Tony's mother was sitting down to the family organ. Devaney lifted his Irish tenor in song, and Arizona never had a chance. "After that," sighs Tony, "there was never a doubt in my mamma's mind about where I was going to college. I was going to play for that nice Mr. Devaney."

Tilt

Devaney's recruiting coups have done little to endear him to rival coaches, who grumble that Nebraska is "long on finances and short on academics." That kind of criticism doesn't bother the pro scouts. Devaney already has furnished the pros with twelve players, and this year's crop of Cornhuskers is the most attractive yet. Murmured one awestruck scout, while watching Nebraska take the field: "When they run out there, you can see the field tilt."

THE 1966
ORANGE BOWL

39

Alabama Takes National Title With Win Over Nebraska In Orange Bowl

By JIMMY BURNS
Special to The Miami Herald

MIAMI, January 1, 1966 — Record-breaking Steve Sloan rounded out the New Year's football surprises Saturday night by sparking Alabama to a 39-28 victory over unbeaten Nebraska in the 32nd Orange Bowl Classic before 74,214 and staking a strong claim to the national championship for the Crimson Tide.

Alabama's easily attained victory made its bid for the No. 1 spot in The Associated Press poll valid as No. 1 Michigan State was upset by U.C.L.A. in the Rose Bowl, 14-12, and Arkansas, ranked second, lost to Louisiana State, 14-7, in the Cotton Bowl. The Associated Press poll will be released Tuesday. Michigan State has already won the United Press International final poll.

Sloan's performance of completing 20 of 29 passes for 296 yards set Orange Bowl records. This plus his aggressive performance gave the senior quarterback the most valuable player award by a landslide vote.

Alabama end Ray Perkins caught nine passes for 159 yards — setting an Orange Bowl record.

Sloan's 20 completions topped the 18 thrown by injured Joe Namath who came off the Alabama bench last January 1 in a heroic, but vain attempt to stop Texas' 21-17 victory. Sloan's yardage bettered the 276 yards by Frank Broyles for Georgia Tech against Tulsa in 1945.

Sloan's passes netted only two touchdowns against Bob Churchich's three scoring passes and 232 yards on 12 completions out of 17 tries for Nebraska.

But the big thing was that Sloan's strong right-arm pitching made shambles of the heavier Cornhuskers' defense. The passing set the Crimson Tide rolling to an easy victory which gave Alabama its second here in four years against the loss only to the Longhorns.

Alabama turned the game into a mismatch as it passed over and ran around the Cornhuskers to gain a 24-7 lead at halftime. It was the biggest intermission margin for an Orange Bowl team since Colorado led Clemson, 20-0, at halftime in 1957.

Alabama finished 9-1-1 and the losers 10-1.

The Crimson Tide set team records with 29 first downs against the 25 the Tide compiled against Syracuse in 1953. Nebraska tied the most points for a loser, 28 by Georgia against Texas in 1949.

Sloan hit Perkins with scoring passes of 21 and 11 yards, plus a two-point conversion. Fullback Steve Bowman, Alabama's leading rusher of 1965, added two touchdowns on plunges of one and three yards while Leslie Kelley scored from four yards out.

Nebraska end Tony Jeter caught two touchdown passes from Churchich for 33 and 14 yards. Ben Gregory took a 49-yard touchdown pass. Churchich added the other touchdown with a one-yard run.

The Cornhuskers struck hard early on the ground, gaining a first down when Ron Kirkland swept around right end on a pitchout. Harry Wilson smashed left tackle for six yards, but he fumbled and Tom Somerville recovered at 'Bama's 39.

Sloan directed the Crimson Tide 69 yards in eight plays, including three passes, to put six points on the scoreboard with 9:36 remaining in the first quarter.

The drive was fused by Sloan's pass to Jerry Duncan on a tackle-eligible tackle play for 17 yards. The touchdown came on a pass to Perkins on the north side of the field. He almost fell, but recovered after his hand touched the ground at the 9-yard line. David Ray kicked the extra point and Alabama led, 7-0.

'Bama tried an onside kickoff, but it backfired by not going the required 10 yards and was recovered by Frank Canterbury at his 36. Ray had kicked from Nebraska's 45 because of a personal foul on the extra-point try. Kirkland busted through right tackle for 27 yards to set off a drive which ended in a futile 20-yard field goal try by Larry Wachholtz.

'Bama drove 71 yards to a first down at the Cornhuskers' six, but Nebraska's defense tightened. On fourth down from the three, Ray was wide to the left with a 19-yard field goal attempt.

Nebraska later tied the score with 12:15 left in the half. Wachholtz signaled for a fair catch of a punt at 'Bama's 48 and the Tide's Dennis Homan grabbed him after the catch.

This gave the Cornhuskers the ball at Alabama's 33 and Churchich, who had been warming up on the sidelines, came in and hit Tony Jeter at the 20 with a pass which he converted into the touchdown. Wachholtz made it 7-7 with his kick.

Despite a 15-yard penalty, Sloan's passing swept the Tide to its second touchdown, eating up 89 yards with 13 plays. The big one was a diving catch of a pass for 39 yards by Perkins at Nebraska's 12. Bowman exploded through the line for eight yards and Les Kelley hit right guard for the touchdown. Ray's kick gave Alabama a 14-7 edge with 7:11 remaining in the second quarter.

Sloan kept the ball in the air except for one short buck by Canterbury as the Tide moved 93 yards in nine plays for its third touchdown. It came when Sloan passed 11 yards to Perkins for the touchdown and Ray made it 21-7 with 1:34 left in the half.

The aggressive Tidesmen tried an onside kick which Vernon Newhill recovered at Nebraska's 46. Sloan hit Perkins with a 35-yard pass, and four plays later Ray kicked an 18-yard field goal with 38 seconds remaining in the half.

'Bama's Canterbury recovered another onside kick at Nebraska's 46. Wachholtz intercepted Sloan's pass, ending a streak of 115 in a row without an interception.

With 10:35 left in the third quarter, Churchich hit Ben Gregory with a 48-yard scoring pass. Ray broke up Wayne Werber's two-point pass attempt and Alabama led, 24-13.

Alabama struck back with Kelley's 25-yard run to launch a retaliatory drive. Bowman got the last yard at left guard and Sloan passed to Perkins for two points and a 32-13 margin with 4:29 left in the period.

Nebraska reached Alabama's one-yard line as the third quarter ended. Churchich scored on the first play of the fourth quarter. Wachholtz's kick reduced Alabama's lead to 32-20.

With 8:13 left in the game, Bowman's 3-yard plunge and Ray's kick boosted the margin to 39-20. A 14-yard pass from Churchich to Jeter and a two-point conversion pass to Gregory reduced the deficit to 39-28 with 2:50 remaining. Most of the fans were on their way home by then.

SCORE BY PERIODS

Alabama 7	17	8	7	—	39
Nebraska 0	7	6	15	—	28

THE 1967
SUGAR BOWL

40

A Bitter Harvest For
The Sugar-Bound Huskers

By JOE JARES
Sports Illustrated

NEW YORK, December 5, 1966 — The question of which teams would meet in the Sugar Bowl on January 2 was about as hush-hush a topic as Lyndon Johnson's hernia-scar operation. Even the Bohemian farmers near the Platte River and the slaughterhouse workers in Omaha knew last week that Nebraska had been invited. The beloved Cornhuskers had gone through nine straight games without a loss or tie (sorry, Ara), they had clinched the Big Eight championship, and the Sugar was the only major bowl left unprogrammed. Still Coach Bob Devaney, an impish Irishman, kept mum until his weekly Extra Point Club luncheon in Lincoln. In a crowded banquet room he accepted the formal invitation from a Sugar Bowl emissary and got on the phone (hooked up to a loudspeaker) with officials of New Orleans' Mid-Winter Sports Association, who told him, just as if the newspapers had not been assuming it for days, that undefeated, untied Alabama also had accepted a bid. Devaney hesitated a moment and then said, "I was afraid of that."

He was joshing, of course, just as he had been earlier when he said the opponent would be the Massachusetts Institute of Technology. Nebraska's Big Red was anxious to play Alabama and avenge the 39-28 loss to the Crimson Tide in last season's Orange Bowl. Both teams had strutted into that game unbeaten, but Alabama came out with the victory and the national title. So the January 2 rematch was a natural.

Nebraska again was cutting down opponents like a row of cornstalks. In the romp over Utah State, safety Larry Wachholtz, only 5-foot-8 and 166 pounds, returned a punt 73 yards for a touchdown, intercepted two passes and kicked a 39-yard field goal. All-America middle guard Wayne Meylan blocked punts against Wisconsin and

Kansas State and turned them both into touchdowns. At Colorado, Nebraska trailed, 19-7, at halftime, but fought back to win, 21-19. After Missouri was harvested, 35-0, Coach Dan Devine said, "I never saw a team with so many big, strong running backs."

No wonder the president of the Mid-Winter Sports Association said, "Without Nebraska we don't have a good intersectional. The people in New Orleans want to see Nebraska in the worst way."

But before the Big Red could start plotting against Alabama, there was one more regular-season chore, the matter of a Thanksgiving Day game down in Norman against Oklahoma. There, before about 6½ million homes tuned in on TV, fourth-ranked Nebraska lost by one frustrating point to a team that was only No. 4 in the Big Eight — and a little sweetness went out of the Sugar Bowl.

Not that Nebraska coaches, players or fans had overlooked Oklahoma. All remembered the agony two years ago, when the Huskers were undefeated fat cats and already selected for the Cotton Bowl. A stopover in Norman resulted in a 17-7 defeat. Also, there were those millions of turkey-stuffed people to impress, not to mention voters in the polls. "It's the 10th game, and we've won nine already," said Meylan. "If we don't win this one it isn't a good season. I don't think anybody is looking beyond to the Sugar Bowl."

Meylan is one of the players who was most respected in advance by Oklahoma. He went into the game with 35 unassisted tackles, 36 assisted tackles and three blocked punts. It was too bad there were no statistics for havoc wreaked.

"The fact that Meylan is so good at so many things presents special problems," said Sooner center Bob Craig. "For one thing, he has big, strong arms and can throw you around. He also has exceptional movement for his size. . . . You don't try to horse him out of there."

Meylan, 6-foot-1, 237 pounds, grew up on his father's navy-bean farm outside Bay City, Mich. And it was there, lifting weights under a tree, throwing fertilizer sacks around and hoeing in the bean fields day after day, that he developed his blacksmith's arms. Last year he could hardly wait for the Thanksgiving Day game to be over so that he could get home to the farm. His father had bought a new tractor, and to Wayne it had twice the allure that a diamond-studded Ferrari would have for almost anybody else. Meylan had another exciting trip planned after this year's Oklahoma game. One of the selectors of all-America teams was flying him back to New York City, his first visit there. He was not worried about meeting muggers — he happens to be Nebraska's intramural heavyweight wrestling champ.

For Oklahoma, the scary thing about Meylan was that he might not be the best of Devaney's linemen. Offensive tackle Bob Pickens, 274 pounds, could block a threshing machine and was an Olympic wrestler in 1964. Defensive tackle Carel Stith has made more tackles than Meylan, and offensive guard LaVerne Allers is just as talented.

Skill and brawn, however, were not left to do everything by Nebraska; superstition has its semi-serious place. The football coaches were careful to repeat previously successful rituals. Two nights before the game — it had to be two — Devaney and several of his assistants met with friends at the Elks Club in Lincoln to consume chicken-liver hors d'oeuvres. Later, with their wives, they met in line coach George Kelly's basement for cocktails, turkey and ham sandwiches and pumpkin cream pie. Nor was the lucky-penny board neglected. The first lucky penny was found before a 1962 victory, and there had been 31 pennies since, plus some dimes and a brass button, all now taped to a piece of cardboard and taken to all games. The night before the Oklahoma game a member of the Nebraska staff found a battered penny in the hotel parking lot.

Oklahoma had no good-luck charms to speak of, but it did have the lean, mean look of a half-starved guerrilla band. Coach Jim Mackenzie worked his players so hard last spring that collectively they lost 1,437 pounds in seven weeks, and no one quit or died of malnutrition. The skinny Sooners started with four straight victories, but Notre Dame took them apart in the fifth game, 38-0. Still, Mackenzie said, they worked themselves like galley slaves in practice the following week. And they labored just as hard after close, deflating losses to Colorado and Missouri.

On Thanksgiving afternoon the stands were full of Nebraskans who had forsaken TV and turkey and traveled 450 miles to witness the hoped-for 10th straight win. They were decked out in red hats, red socks, red dresses and red everything else, including red faces after the first play of the game. Oklahoma's Eddie Hinton returned the kickoff 59 yards, but a fumble on the second play from scrimmage killed that threat. Early in the second quarter, Nebraska ended a drive from its own nine with a 28-yard Larry Wachholtz field goal that just dribbled over the crossbar. Then it was Oklahoma's turn. The Sooners went ahead, 7-3, on a 48-yard touchdown pass from Bob Warmack

119

to Hinton, who made a fine leaping catch, and Mike Vachon's extra-point kick. Throughout, Oklahoma's offensive linemen were rudely rejecting the attempts of Wayne Meylan (or anyone else) to get into their backfield. Often they were double-teaming Meylan.

Nebraska finally put together a complete drive in the third quarter, moving 80 yards in 13 plays for a touchdown, but a bad pass from center enabled Sooner Bob Stephenson to block Wachholtz's extra-point try. Nebraska 9, Oklahoma 7. An Oklahoma field goal would win the game. The team got close enough early in the fourth period, but Mike Vachon's 23-yard boot was wide to the left, and he went back to the sideline looking for a suicide pistol. Coach Mackenzie told him, "Forget it! We'll give you another chance."

Mackenzie was almost wrong, but, on a gutty drive from their own 24, the Sooners took the ball deep into Nebraska territory. Three times on the drive they faced long yardage on third down, and three times they made it. With 48 seconds left Vachon got his other chance. His aim was true this time. He kicked the ball through the goal posts from the 11-yard line. The Okies led, 10-9. As it had done so often this season, Nebraska came straight back upfield, but the drive, like three others this day, ended ignominiously, this time with an interception. The loss was the third in three tries against three different coaches for Bob Devaney's teams at Norman.

Among Oklahomans, after the upset, there was happy chatter about a possible postseason excursion of their own. It is not to be, unfortunately, and there is still Oklahoma State to play. But Mackenzie was not thinking of other games. "Fifty-four million people watchin' this one," he said, "and it's gettin' near recruitin' time."

In the Cornhusker dressing room a disappointed New Orleans representative insisted, "As far as I'm concerned, they're still Big Eight champions, and they'll be received as well as ever." He gave Devaney a Sugar Bowl invitation engraved in metal and mounted on polished wood. The original idea was to make the presentation before a joyous, and undefeated, Nebraska squad. But as their coach accepted the plaque, the tired, gloomy athletes did not even look around.

41

Alabama Routs Nebraska In Sugar Bowl

By BOB ROESLER
Special to The New Orleans Times-Picayune

NEW ORLEANS, January 2, 1967 — Nebraska found there is no substitute for speed Monday as racehorse-swift Alabama ripped to a 34-7 victory in the 33rd edition of the Sugar Bowl before a sellout crowd of 82,000.

Alabama quarterback Ken (Snake) Stabler utilized the quickness of his receivers and jet-like leatherluggers and had the Crimson Tide on top of all of the breaks.

For his efforts Stabler was awarded The Miller-Digby Award for the Sugar Bowl's most valuable player in a landslide.

There were many 'Bama heroes this damp, foggy afternoon. Steve Davis was one, contributing field goals of 30 and 40 yards plus 4 extra points.

Another was all-American end Ray Perkins who scored on a 43-yard pass from Stabler and caught six more aerials for a total of 178 yards.

Still another was defensive tackle Louis Thompson, who was a thorn — no, make that a spike — in the sides of Nebraska ballcarriers.

And the play of defensive halfback Bobby Johns, whose three interceptions knotted a Sugar Bowl record.

But all of 'em had to take a back seat to Stabler, who became the ninth quarterback to win the M.V.P. hardware. The trigger-happy Stabler, who completed a 45-yard pass to Perkins on the very first play from scrimmage, hit on 12 of 18 passes. In so doing, Stabler, the junior from Foley, Ala., picked up 218 yards. He also carried nine times for 38 more yards, for a total yardage of 256 yards.

Bob Churchich hit on 21 of 34 passes for 201 yards, four of them coming in the last minutes of play when Nebraska was firing desperation shots in a vain effort to close the gap on the Alabamans.

The Cornhusker ground attack could penetrate Alabama's tough defense for only 84 yards, with sub fullback Dick Davis as Nebraska's top man with 37 yards on 10 carries.

Bear Bryant, attempting to latch on to the coveted Grantland Rice Trophy, which is awarded annually to the nation's top team by the Football Writers Association of America, swept his bench from one end to the other.

He was forced to sub at fullback early in the game when Les Kelley, who got 'Bama's first TD, left the game with a shoulder injury.

A light, but steady rain fell before noon, but by kickoff time only the fog kept the day from being letter-perfect. The field, but for one spot at the 10-yard line at the north end of the field, was in excellent condition. It had been protected by a tarp for the past rain-swept days.

Stabler didn't waste any time in jolting the Nebraskans. Mike Sasser returned the kickoff to the 'Bama 28. Then on the very first play Stabler, with all of the time in the world to throw, lofted an aerial to Ray Perkins who was at the Cornhusker 40. The all-America end made an easy catch and wasn't knocked to the turf until he had reached the Nebraska 27.

The super sensational play covered 45 yards.

On the next play Stabler fed the pigskin to fullback Les Kelley and he burst up the middle for another first down at the 17. Snake gained two more, then hit Perkins with a 6-yarder to the 9.

Les Kelley torpedoed his way over from the three to activate the scoreboard after less than five minutes of action. Steve Davis' extra point made it 7-6.

After Nebraska was unable to move, the Tide raced 71 yards on four plays to make it 14-0 with 7:23 left in the opening period. The big play was a 44-yard aerial from Stabler to dependable Perkins for a first down at Nebraska's 20.

Snake came right back with a 6-yarder to Dennis Homan. On the next play Stabler crossed 'em up by skirting left end for the TD. Not a foul came within feet of the Alabama flash. Davis was on target with his kick and the score was now 14-0. The highly publicized Tide defenses kept the Huskers completely bottled up and the Nebraskans had to punt the next time they got a chance at the ball.

But 'Bama couldn't move after the punt, and they, too, ordered a kick. The Nebraskans were at their own 39 when Harry Wilson fumbled and Charley Harris recovered for the Tide at that spot.

A sensational 21-yard run by Stabler, when seemingly hopelessly stopped, set up another Alabama score. The run, aided by a key block from Dave Chatwood, put the ball on Nebraska's 12.

When three plays lost a couple of yards, Bryant raced in Davis to attempt a field goal from the 20. The 30-yard kick was true and the score read 17-0, Alabama, with 28 seconds left in the first quarter.

Bryant was substituting freely in the first quarter using 35 white-shirted warriors against the heavy Nebraskans.

The second period was in its infancy when Trimble took over for Stabler. A 9-yard pass to Homan and a 13-yard canter by halfback Ed Morgan brought it to Nebraska's 49. On the next play Trimble was in more trouble than the law allowed. Harassed by three charging Nebraskans he managed to hit John Reitz with a shot which Reitz somehow managed to hold on to. Reitz broke away from one tackler, but was finally brought down at the 18.

'Bama moved it to the nine. Then while facing a fourth and one, Ed Morgan crashed to the seven for a first and goal.

Two plays later Trimble skirted left end. He stiff-armed one tormentor at the two and went into the end zone standing up. With 7:03 left in the period Davis' kick made it 24-0.

The first half was just one minute away from history when the Cornhuskers finally knew what Alabama territory looked like. Churchich completed a dazzling 26-yard pass to Harry Wilson for a first down at Alabama's 38. Four plays later they had advanced just nine yards and had to surrender the ball to the Red Elephants.

Seconds later the half ended, the proud Alabamans heading for the locker room with that 24-0 bulge, a score the Alabama band quickly, but expertly, spelled out on the field during a colorful half-time show.

The Bear used 43 players in the first half to bury the Huskers under an impressive pile of statistics. The Tuscaloosa Terrors gained 113 yards by land and 164 by air. They ran 25 plays to Nebraska's 14.

Nebraska had to settle for 43 yards on the ground and 70 on Churchich's arm. In the first down department, it was Alabama, 11-5.

Alabama had a mild chance at a TD early in the third period when Bobby Johns intercepted a Churchich pass at midfield. But three plays netted nothing and Davis punted to Wachholtz at the 13 and the Nebraska all-America hauled it back to the 20.

A 33-yard sweep of right end by Ben Gregory and a 14-yard pass from Churchich to Davis gave Nebraska the ball on Alabama's 38.

But Johns came up with another interception, this time at the Tide 16.

From there, Stabler moved the Tide to a field goal, the big play being a 27-yard pass to Perkins, putting the ball on the Nebraska 27.

After Snake was smeared for a nine-yard loss, he got 13 yards on a run off a broken pass play to get the ball to the 23.

On the next play Steve Davis booted a field goal from the 36 to make it 27-0 with a shade better than two minutes left in the third quarter.

Nebraska seemed to smell points as they began clicking through the air with Churchich hitting Dennis Richnafsky several times and Miles Kimmel and Charley Winters.

The series of shots brought Nebraska to the Tide 19, their deepest penetration of the afternoon.

Churchich finally got some points with a 15-yard toss to Dick Davis, the TD coming just five seconds into the fourth period. Wachholtz kicked the extra point to make it 27-7.

Stabler then decided to try the spectacular to redeem things for the Tide defensive unit, calling upon his all-America end, Perkins.

With the ball on Nebraska's 45, Stabler faded back to pass, shook off a few onrushing Cornhusker linemen and sighted Perkins at Nebraska's 30. He took the pass in, shook loose one tackler, dodged another, then out-legged two weary-legged Nebraskans, going the last 20 yards with ease.

Steve Davis kicked the point-after and, with 11:33 left, the score was now 34-7.

With six minutes left Johns picked off his third Nebraska pass, this one thrown by Wayne Weber. Johns picked it off at the 'Bama 23 and ran it back to the 38.

The last minutes of the game were filled with activity. Alabama intercepted two desperate Nebraska heaves. The Huskers got the ball back on a fumble recovery after an interception and went to throwing wildly.

Churchich completed five of six passes to move Nebraska to Alabama's 14 with just 27 seconds left. But on the next play Nebraska fumbled and Dick Cole pounced on it to give Alabama the pleasure of having the ball at the game's end.

When the gun finally sounded, Coach Bryant raced out onto the field to shake hands with Nebraska Coach Bob Devaney, then personally got the game-winning football and carried it into the jubilant Tide locker room.

Score By Periods

Alabama 17	7	3	7	—	34
Nebraska 0	0	0	7	—	7

THE 1969
SUN BOWL

42

Nebraska Routs Georgia In Sun Bowl

By UNITED PRESS INTERNATIONAL
The New York Times

EL PASO, Tex., December 20, 1969 — Paul Rogers kicked four field goals in the first quarter and Nebraska scored two touchdowns in less than a minute in the third quarter today to give the Cornhuskers a 45-6 triumph over Georgia in the 35th Sun Bowl game.

Rogers, taking advantage of a favorable 12-mile-an-hour wind, booted field goals of 50, 32, 42 and 37 yards and Jeff Kinney scored on an 11-yard run to give Nebraska an 18-0 lead in the first quarter.

Nebraska, the Big Eight co-champion, put the game out of reach with its scoring spurt in the third quarter. The Cornhusker quarterback, Van Brownson, hit his fullback, Mike Green, from 11 yards out for one touchdown and plunged over from the 1 for the second.

The Cornhuskers' other touchdowns came on a l-yard plunge by Dan Schneiss and a l-yard run by reserve quarterback Jerry Tagge in the fourth quarter.

Georgia, which crossed midfield only three times, scored its touchdown on a 6-yard run by the quarterback, Paul Gilbert, late in the final period.

After Brownson hit Green with the 11-yard touchdown pass in the third quarter, Nebraska got the ball right back when the Cornhuskers intercepted a pass and ran it back 43 yards to the 2, setting up Brownson's run.

The injury-riddled Bulldog offense was completely stopped by Nebraska's "black shirt" defense, which came up with six pass interceptions and two fumbles.

Three of Rogers' field goals were set up by Bulldog mistakes. Rogers, who kicked three field goals of 50 yards or better during the regular season, opened the scoring with a 50-yard boot with 11:14 left in the first quarter.

On the ensuing Georgia drive, the Bulldog fullback, Julian Smiley, fumbled at his own 31 and a Nebraska tackle, Dave Walline, fell on the loose ball on the 31. Six plays later, Rogers booted his second 3-pointer.

Georgia, criticized by some Georgia sports writers for accepting the Sun Bowl bid despite only a 5-4-1 won-lost-tied regular season record, played without its first-string quarterback, Mike Cavan, who was sidelined with injuries suffered late in the season.

The triumph was Nebraska Coach Bob Devaney's second in the Sun Bowl. His 1958 Wyoming squad whipped Hardin-Simmons, 14-6. The loss evened the record of Georgia Coach Vince Dooley in the bowl at 1-1. Georgia's earlier victory at El Paso was a 7-0 upset of Texas Tech in 1964.

Nebraska, a one-touchdown favorite, took an 8-2 won-lost record into the game, including victories over Oklahoma, Colorado and Kansas State. The losses were to Southern California, which is Rose Bowl-bound and Missouri, which will play in the Orange Bowl.

Georgia had victories over South Carolina and Kentucky and a tie with Florida. The Bulldog losses were to Tennessee, Auburn, Georgia Tech and Sugar Bowl-bound Mississippi.

Rogers, selected by sports writers as the game's most valuable player, also kicked three extra-point conversions to finish with 15 points. He surprised the crowd, however, when he missed one conversion attempt.

SCORE BY PERIODS

Nebraska	18	0	14	13 —	45
Georgia	0	0	0	6 —	6

THE 1971
ORANGE BOWL

43

Nebraska Bids For No. 1 By Whipping L.S.U. In Orange Bowl

By BOB ELLIOTT
Special to The Miami Herald

MIAMI, January 1, 1971 — The Dolphins' impossible dream died in the mud of Oakland Stadium last Sunday, but on the Poly-Turf of the Orange Bowl Friday night, an even more unlikely dream took a tremendous step toward reality when Nebraska outlasted Louisiana State, 17-12, in the 37th annual Orange Bowl Classic.

The bitterly-won victory, coming hours after Texas' 24-11 loss to Notre Dame and Ohio State's 27-17 upset at the hands of Stanford, is expected to earn Coach Bob Devaney's unbeaten Cornhuskers the 1970 national collegiate football championship.

The final Associated Press poll, on which the national title is based, will be taken this week and it'll come as a shock if Nebraska doesn't wind up No. 1. In the final poll of the regular season, Texas was No. 1, Ohio State No. 2 and Nebraska No. 3.

The odds on the Notre Dame-Stanford-Nebraska parlay must have been astronomical, but it happened — just as Devaney and his proud charges had hoped it would.

Nebraska winds up its 1970 campaign unbeaten in 12 games, with only a 21-21 tie with Southern California marring its record. The defeat was L.S.U.'s third as against nine triumphs.

A record Orange Bowl crowd of 80,699 watched the powerful Nebraska and L.S.U. clubs wage one of the bitterest fights in the history of the Orange Bowl classic.

It wasn't until less than nine minutes were left in the game that the Cornhuskers managed to push across the touchdown that gave them the lead and the eventual victory.

Nebraska had grabbed a 10-0 first quarter cushion, saw it cut to 10-3 by halftime and vanish entirely on the last play of the third period as L.S.U. clicked on a 31-yard scoring play and a 12-10 advantage.

However, the Cornhuskers weren't about to let slip the opportunity which Notre Dame and Stanford had set up for them.

They ran the following kickoff back to their 33 and went on a 14-play, time-consuming march that culminated in a 1-yard scoring play by quarterback Jerry Tagge. The Cornhusker drive used up six minutes and 10 seconds of the final period and L.S.U. couldn't bounce back in the remaining time.

Tagge, who did most of the quarterbacking for the winners, was voted the game's most valuable back, with the Cornhuskers' fine end, Willie Harper, earning the award as the most valuable lineman.

There wasn't much to choose between the clubs in the final analysis. Each had its great moments as well as its weak periods.

Statistics bear out the closeness of the struggle. L.S.U. had 20 first downs to Nebraska's 18, and 227 yards passing to the Cornhuskers' 161. On the ground Nebraska had the edge, 132 to 51. Total offense figures read 293 for the winners; 278 for the losers.

It was just that close.

Louisiana State was hampered considerably by the loss, early in the first quarter, of its best running back, Art Cantrelle. His replacement, Chris Dantin, did more than an adequate job, but still Cantrelle's absence had to hurt the Tiger ground attack.

The rivals sparred around in the early part of the game, as was expected. The Tigers appeared ready for the first serious bid when they moved from their 20 to Nebraska's 43, but Dantin missed a handoff at that point and Dave Walline, a fine defensive tackle all night, covered for the Cornhuskers.

Nebraska moved from its 43 to the L.S.U. 8, but the Tigers got tough and Paul Rogers kicked a 26-yard field goal to get the Huskers on the scoreboard. Tagge was the big man in the drive, both passing and running.

Thirty-four seconds after Rogers' field goal, Nebraska had its first touchdown and a 10-0 lead.

It came about when L.S.U. quarterback Buddy Lee fumbled on the first play after the kickoff and Harper covered for Nebraska on the Tiger 15. Joe Orduna ran wide for 12 and then smashed through left tackle for the TD. Rogers converted with two minutes still left in the quarter.

After stumbling around for most of the second period, with its passers — Lee and Bert Jones — taking a fierce beating due to poor pass protection, L.S.U. got moving from its 24 yard line.

Andy Hamilton took a 22-yard pass from Lee, then two more shots for 17 and 6 yards to the Nebraska 34. Lee ran for 10 yards to reach the Cornhusker 20 and then got away for 9½. Needing inches for another first down, Lee was caught by Harper for a 10-yard loss. On fourth down, Mark Lumpkin kicked a 37-yard field goal.

Nebraska, however, was guilty of illegal use of hands on the kick and L.S.U. had the choice of taking the field goal or the penalty which would have left it still with inches to go on fourth down.

With only 49 seconds left in the half, Coach Charlie McClendon elected to take the three points already on the board. Nebraska, however, still led, 10-3.

L.S.U. came out of the dressing room ready to play football after the halftime intermission.

Taking the third quarter kick on its 20, L.S.U. sent Dantin roaring for 25 yards on a quick opener. Two plays later, Nebraska's Joe Blahak was guilty of interfering with Hamilton on an incomplete pass and L.S.U. was on the Huskers' 32.

Dantin ran for 17 more, but on third down with a yard to go at the Nebraska 7, Dantin slipped and lost a yard, so Lumpkin booted a 25-yard field goal with 11:49 still left in the period. Nebraska's lead was now narrowed to 10-6.

L.S.U. got another chance almost immediately when Bill Norsworthy intercepted a Nebraska pass on the Tiger 48, but the S.E.C. club couldn't move and had to punt.

Neither club did much until late in the third quarter when L.S.U. launched a 75-yard drive that wound up in its lone touchdown of the night.

Lee hit Hamilton for 16, then roamed off tackle for 10 yards and when Nebraska was penalized for piling on, the Tigers were at the Nebraska 34.

Three plays later, Lee found Al Coffee all alone at the 6-yard line, dropped a perfect pass in his arms and the touchdown was easy. Defender Jim Anderson slipped on the way back to defend making Coffee's simple task an easier one.

135

L.S.U. now led, 12-10. The kick for the extra point failed, leaving Nebraska in a position to win with a field goal.

However, the Cornhuskers weren't thinking field goal.

Taking off from its 33, Nebraska used 10 running plays and four passes to get across the goal. The biggest gainer was a 17-yard aerial from Tagge to Jeff Kinney on the L.S.U. 5.

The Tigers gave in grudgingly, but Tagge finally pushed the ball over the goal from a yard out.

Rogers' conversion produced the night's final scoring and the lead, 17-12.

Not long afterward, it looked as if Nebraska might pad its lead when it reached the L.S.U. 13, but a fumble was covered by the Tigers.

L.S.U. backers got their spirits lifted a bit when Jones hit Hamilton with a 30-yard pass to the Tiger 38, but the quarterback fumbled four plays later and Nebraska's Willie Harper recovered.

That looked to be it, but Tagge dropped the ball with 52 seconds left and L.S.U. got one final shot.

It was a pass from Jones, but it dropped into Nebraska's Bob Terrio's hands on the Cornhusker 38 and "We're No. 1" signs went up all over the Nebraska cheering section.

SCORE BY PERIODS

Nebraska 10	0	0	7	—	17
Louisiana State 0	3	9	0	—	12

44

Nebraska's Dream
Comes True

By THE ASSOCIATED PRESS
The New York Times

MIAMI, January 1, 1971 — "Hell, yes, we're No. 1," Coach Bob Devaney shouted tonight after his Nebraska Cornhuskers scored a hair-raising 17-12 victory over Louisiana State and staked a claim to the national collegiate football championship.

"We're the only undefeated team, I can't see how the Pope himself could vote for Notre Dame," Devaney said in the wild atmosphere of a jubilant dressing room.

Cries of "We're No. 1," rang from the Cornhusker cheering section throughout the last quarter of a game that was undecided until Bob Terrio intercepted a pass with less than a minute to go.

And when the Huskers, yelling and pummeling each other, ran into the dressing room, the Nebraska band stood outside and delivered lusty serenades.

'A Dream Come True'

"It was a dream come true," said Jerry Tagge, the quarterback.

He referred to the day's earlier defeats of No. 1 Texas by Notre Dame and No. 2 Ohio State by Stanford, smashing upsets that put the national title on the line in the Orange Bowl.

Tagge, who scored the winning touchdown on a 1-yard plunge in the fourth quarter, said Devaney told him to "run anything I wanted" in the drive.

But he said Devaney "told us we didn't necessarily have to throw deep."

"We thought we could beat them deep," Tagge said, "but it didn't work out that way."

"You're damned right we're No. 1," yelled Larry Jacobson, a

defensive tackle. "Nobody would believe us the whole year, but we finally proved it."

They're No. 1 With Fans

Before the game, the longest telegram ever delivered by Western Union came to the team from fans in Nebraska. In contained 46,200 signatures. Unrolled, it was 1,400 feet long.

The message read:

"Congratulations and best wishes to the finest coaching staff and players in America. You are No. 1 with us. We are very proud of you. Go, Big Red."

"We ran on them," said Dan Schneiss, the fullback. "That's something nobody else could do all year."

Nebraska rushed for 132 yards against the nation's No. 1 defense.

A sturdy defensive back and rugged tackler, Larry Wachholtz (36) was a popular choice on all-America teams in 1966.

Cornhusker quarterback Jerry Tagge, a sophomore in 1969, breaks loose for big yardage against Missouri.

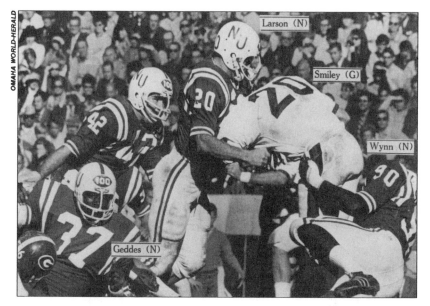

Nebraska's Al Larson (20) and Mike Wynn (90) stop Georgia's Julian Smiley (20) in the 1969 Sun Bowl. The Cornhuskers won this contest rather convincingly, 45-6.

In the Sun Bowl, Bulldog defenders spent most of the afternoon chasing down Jerry Tagge (14) and the other members of Nebraska's potent offense.

Nebraska opened the 1970 season by defeating Wake Forest, 36-12, and tying U.S.C., 21-21. Against Army, Tagge led the Cornhuskers to a 28-0 victory.

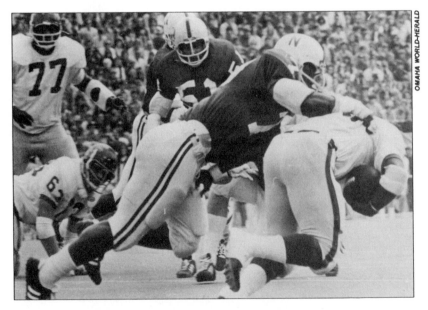

Rich Glover was a two-time all-American at nose guard for the Cornhuskers in 1971 and 1972. In 1972, he finished 3d in the balloting for the Heisman Trophy.

All-America defensive lineman Larry Jacobson proved to be a big threat to opposing quarterbacks in 1971.

In the Game of the Century against the Sooners, played in Norman, Okla., Johnny Rodgers' punt return for a touchdown was the decisive play.

45

Cornhuskers Came Bombing

By EDWIN POPE
Special to The Miami Herald

MIAMI, January 1, 1971 — The Orange Bowl came out smelling like a rose.

If Nebraska isn't No. 1, there isn't any justice.

The coldest Orange Bowl Classic in nine years turned into the hottest in a lot longer than that. Nebraska's 17-12 nudging of Louisiana State should entitle the Cornhuskers to dance over the beaten bodies of Texas and Ohio State and into the topmost national ranking to be announced early next week.

Bob Devaney's Big Eight Conference champions skipped off the artificial turf with fingers raised to signify No. 1. They have it coming.

That national title would be a beautiful climax to a match that looked like the berries from the day it was made but, strangely, failed to arouse the usual enthusiasm among the citizenry.

The lack of early public excitement probably was due to the Dolphins late drive and the pro championships coming up Sunday. But it didn't show in the record crowd of 80,699 in the great horseshoe Friday night.

I got an idea I was watching one of Bud Wilkinson's old Oklahoma outfits as the Cornhuskers in their blood-red suits whisked up and down the Orange Bowl rug.

They were quick. They were poised. And they weren't operating against any patsies. L.S.U. was as savage defensively as advertised and hung in there all the way despite erratic quarterbacking.

To be fair to the Tiger quarterbacks, Bert Jones and Buddy Lee, they spent much of the 55-degree evening with Nebraska rushers stuck to their helmets.

In the first half, Tiger quarterbacks were sacked six times for losses totaling 65 yards. L.S.U. finished the first half with a rushing aggregate of minus 45 yards. It seemed as miraculous that they were behind only 10-3, just as Missouri only being beaten by that score by Penn State a year ago despite seven interceptions.

There is a gathering mass of opinion that the Big Eight plays the best football top-to-bottom of any conference in the country, including the Southeastern.

The Cornhuskers did nothing to weaken that notion Friday night.

The original surprise was Nebraska coming out throwing. They had the man to do it, a crisply named junior quarterback, Jerry Tagge. He was the one who got Nebraska off fast and then furnished the finishing kick after Louisiana State had gone ahead at 12-10 on the last play of the third quarter.

The Cornhuskers had built their 10-0-1 regular-season record on an irresistible ground force. But Tagge entered the arena with bombs on his mind. He hit on 6 of 10 passes in the first quarter as Nebraska dazed L.S.U. with a 10-0 lead in that period.

To Charlie McClendon some flowers for waking up the Tigers at halftime. He must have invoked shades of Huey Long, or somebody, in the L.S.U. bathhouse.

The Tigers came back winging from a 10-3 halftime deficit. Or perhaps Nebraska simply was softened by its band's intermission presentation of a "Love" theme.

Whatever the case, when L.S.U. stomped ahead, 12-10, that put it squarely up to Nebraska to behave like a No. 1 team should.

The Cornhuskers did it just that way. They plowed 67 yards and over to start the fourth quarter, with Tagge scoring their second ground touchdown against an L.S.U. defense that had allowed only that many scores rushing the entire season.

The goat of the game could have been L.S.U.'s Mark Lumpkin. Unaccountably his conversion attempt after the Tigers went ahead, 12-10, skittered off to the side.

Lumpkin had made good on 32 of 34 extra points during the regular season. Yet this miss could have allowed Nebraska to win by 13-12 with just a field goal.

The Cornhuskers were kindly enough, in their otherwise vicious approach, to take the monkey off young Lumpkin's back by scoring a touchdown rather than a field goal. The Cornhuskers then led, 17-12.

Those five points made an accurate reflection of the difference between two superbly prepared teams.

I thought that as a twosome they were the strongest teams to meet in the Orange Bowl since Oklahoma beat Maryland, 7-0, here in 1954.

That's a long time but these were two hairy bunches.

Now the rankings people can put a proper lid on a real classic by naming Nebraska the best college football team in America.

THE LEGEND OF
BOB DEVANEY

46

And This Man Is At The Top

By JOHN UNDERWOOD
Sports Illustrated

NEW YORK, September 13, 1971 — When Bob Devaney of Nebraska tells the true story of Bob Devaney's climb to the top of the coaching profession, all the lightning strokes of genius are left out. The gaffes, however, glow like zircons in the chronology of his account. It is Devaney's style to remind you that in the first game in which he played for little Alma (Mich.) College in 1936 he had three teeth knocked out, cleanly, and that he never intended to become a coach at all. He was an economics major. Some economics majors learn more than others. He left Alma owing the school $350 and had to wait tables, pump gas and sweep the gym floor to finish that close to even.

Picking up the thread from there, Devaney says that when he was the baseball coach at Saginaw (Mich.) High he had a pitcher named Bob Buhl who, Devaney concluded, could not pitch in that cool Michigan weather. In a spasm of inspiration, Devaney converted Buhl into a weak-hitting first baseman. Buhl eventually converted back and went on to become a big winner with the Milwaukee Braves during their glory days in the late 50's. "That," says Bob Devaney, "tells you the kind of baseball coach I was."

At Big Beaver High in Birmingham, Mich., his first stop after graduating from Alma, Devaney also coached football and basketball and taught six subjects a day — civics, history, biology, etc. On the basis of a 60 to 70 hour week, he once told *The Omaha World-Herald* he made 50¢ an hour and deserved every penny. He said that the kids of Big Beaver "did not have much interest in athletics." The football team had not won a game in four years and the turnout was so sparse Devaney had to scrimmage with the players. His basketball team practiced in a gym, but the gym was in another town and Devaney's wife, Phyllis, took a teaching job to help pay for a car to take the team to practice. "We did not win any state championships in basketball," said Devaney. "I remember the car better than I do the basketball team."

Once paid for, the car was demolished when intersected by a streetcar in downtown Detroit. "We weren't sly enough to pretend we were injured and sue the streetcar company for $50,000," Devaney said. "All we got out of it was $25 for the car."

Devaney said he found out at Big Beaver how little he knew about football coaching. He discovered there was more to it than you block that man and you block this one. After that he moved around Michigan some, to Saginaw to Keego Harbor, logging coaching years, and wound up at Alpena High, hard by Lake Huron where the cold mist settles on a fall night and where he won a remarkable 52 of 61 games with athletes who disappeared back into the mist and were never heard from again. Asked if any of those could have become successful college players, Devaney replied: "Dick So-and-So was a great athlete at Alpena and would have been outstanding in college except he wouldn't go to class."

Devaney had been a coach 14 years and seemed on his way to that special purgatory for highly respected, grossly underpaid career high school coaches when he was summoned to Michigan State, "where my real life began." He was a shot in the dark, he says. Duffy Daugherty called on a summer afternoon "when I just happened to be in from the lake. If he had not reached me, he'd have called somebody else. I have no illusions about that. But I had made up my mind. I was 37. If a break didn't come before I was 40 I was going to go back and get my Masters and take a boring administrative job somewhere."

Eventually, Devaney got another call (he was 41 then) to become head coach at the University of Wyoming where he continued the tradition of winning teams by accident, of course, and was lauded and loved and given a "lifetime contract." He said the secret of his success at Wyoming was being able to bring in some renegade athletes to go with a few incumbent "orangatangs" — he used the word affectionately — who could play the game. He said the president was sympathetic to his needs. The president was from the South and used to talk about the good old days when college players got paid off behind the chicken coop. It was, however, no easy task to keep prospects in Laramie once they set foot there, so Devaney stationed coaches at the airport and bus and railroad depots in case anyone decided to keep going after taking a look around.

"I learned to love Wyoming, but I had some embarrassing moments," says Devaney. One of his harder-headed players, a New Yorker, refused to show his I.D. card to a policeman when approached while lounging in a hotel lobby one night before a game. A row started. Devaney and a few others interceded, and "we all got taken down to the station. I offered a sound defense argument and about had it all straightened out, too, when I pressed my luck. They said the player would have to stay in jail overnight. I said, 'If he stays, we all stay.' So they locked us up. It was headlines the next day."

The road back to Laramie from recruiting trips and late-ending banquets was treacherous, Devaney said. One night he dozed off and his university-owned automobile, left to its own devices, headed down the side of a cliff. "I thought I was driving hell out of it, too, and when we got to the bottom and I got out to look at the car I realized we had rolled over three or four times." Abashed, he explained to the administration that a deer had run across his path.

Devaney declared his life over at Wyoming in 1962 and accepted the challenge at Nebraska. By now he was 46 years old, but as Pepper Rodgers of U.C.L.A. says, "Devaney's young, no matter how old he is." Soon Devaney had a reputation for being a fantastic recruiter. He says it was nothing special, he was just loath to deprive a boy of the opportunity of playing football in Nebraska just because he happened to live on Long Island. He made Nebraska a national institution. A smart, exceptionally quick-witted man, he could talk crop rotation with farmers and profit and loss with financiers — if their sons were football players. He says he found recruiting very educational. In a West Virginia tenement one night he sat in the living room listening to the mother of a hot prospect play "Bringing in the Sheaves" on the family piano.

"Is it true," Devaney was asked, "that you have gone so far as to sing hymns with a mother to get her boy to go to Nebraska?"

"Yes, I did that," Devaney replied. "The mother came to Nebraska and the boy enrolled at Missouri."

Turning back six years of intransigent failure at football at Nebraska,

Devaney took his very first team of Cornhuskers to an 9-2 record and the Gotham Bowl, where Miami's George Mira passed them silly for 320 yards. Still, Nebraska won, 36-34. "You have made me famous," Devaney told his team. "I've received a number of offers to lecture on defense."

For the first time in his long life as a coach, Devaney says, he began to get national recognition. A magazine writer from the East came out and took one look at Devaney's original wardrobe, his cavalier disregard for fit, his unique color blending, and compared him to Willy Loman in *Death of a Salesman*. Devaney announced that he was furious. "Tell that guy I'm going to sue him and his magazine for defamation," he said. Then he smiled. "Of course, he will be able to offer the perfect defense. The truth."

Devaney got a lot of mileage out of that episode at subsequent gatherings of press people where, invariably, he was chided about his now publicized lack of style. "I won't say the writer drank a lot while he was out here, although it was mostly my liquor," he says, "but a terrible thing happened. After he wrote the story he died. They cremated him and it took three days to put out the flame."

Now, in the fall of his 33d year of coaching, the Bob Devaney of Big Beaver, Alpena and Laramie, the same Bob Devaney who tells these un-Homeric stories that endear him to friends and luncheon audiences across the country, is the same Bob Devaney who keeps coaches like Vince Gibson awake nights. Gibson is the coach at Kansas State and he says he wakes up at 2:30 in the morning and tries to read a book and can't because all he can think about is "how are we going to beat Nebraska?" It's all Devaney's fault, Gibson says.

Looking back, through the mists and over the cliffs of his stumbling-ever-upward pursuit of the laureate, it is now clear that under Devaney Nebraska would inevitably win a national championship, which it did last New Year's night by defeating L.S.U. in the Orange Bowl to climax an unbeaten season. Even then, Devaney was reluctant to leave well enough alone. Notre Dame had knocked off top-ranked Texas in the Cotton Bowl that afternoon. Though the Irish had lost a game and Nebraska had only one tie against its record, Notre Dame's Ara Parseghian lobbied for his team as No. 1 on the grounds of its having accepted "the greater challenge." "Not even the Pope could vote for Notre Dame," Devaney said. Parseghian leaped on the remark, calling it "poor taste." Devaney, alas, had succeeded in riling the Catholics.

"I was afraid Ara's comments might influence the vote, but the writers were too smart to take some coach's word," said Devaney, his Irish blue eyes smiling after The Associated Press picked Nebraska No. 1 anyway. "Coaches don't know anything about rankings."

The fact slips up on you, but Bob Devaney — that unpretentious, unassuming man, that bored pleasant potato face, that dumpy baker's build — is now the winningest coach in college football. Which is to say that among those with at least 10 years' experience he has won with greater regularity than anyone, a .791 percentage on 114 victories, 28 losses and six ties. Actually, Devaney has been the winningest, the president of the lodge, for six years, and the members below him have neon names like Bryant and Hayes and McKay and Royal. And Parseghian.

To tell of the transformation of Nebraska football since he came is to tell of a man working a miracle, a resurrection from the dead. Out of the depths of 17 losing seasons in the previous 21 under his predecessors, the Cornhuskers have soared to nine straight winning seasons under Devaney. In those previous 21 years they went to one bowl game; Devaney has taken them to seven. They have twice had undefeated regular seasons; before that, the last unbeaten Nebraska team was in 1915. They have won or shared six Big Eight championships, and Devaney has been conference Coach of the Year four times. Big Ten teams that used to come to Lincoln to give Nebraska lessons in the sport came and were themselves strongly rebuked; they have lost nine out of nine in games with Devaney's teams, and by such scores as 42-14 and 37-0.

Sepulchral old Memorial Stadium, built on the Lincoln campus in 1923, has seen three additions, a handsome new press box and a $250,000 counterpane of Astroturf since Devaney, and every bolt and synthetic thread is being paid for out of athletic department funds. The team averages more than 67,000 fans a game (fourth highest in the nation). All home games are sold out in January. Season tickets are precious jewels, impossible to beg or borrow. The story is told of friends of a deceased season ticket holder dropping by the house after the funeral to check on the disposition of his seats. It is an old story, but in the case of Nebraska probably true.

And rather than miss a game, a millionaire fan named F.L. Cappart flies in from Vicksburg, Miss., in his private jet every week. Cappart has been known to drop everything to fly to Lincoln for a kickoff. Once when he dropped everything he was in Turkey.

Devaney was chosen Man of the Year, 1970, by *The Omaha World-Herald*, which defended the choice by pointing out that 1970 "was a year people needed something . . . solid to rely on." Chancellor D.B. Varner said it was his job to make the university as good in education as Devaney had made it in football. Support clubs and "beef clubs" sprang up like cornstalks throughout the state, contributing thousands to the million-dollar football budget and tons of raw meat to the team training table. On "O" street in downtown Lincoln, a plain Jane town of 150,000 in the Nebraska breadbasket, a fan could buy a rug, a sticker, a pen, a paperweight, or a whiskey bottle in the form of a "1," or a "Go, Big Red" wristwatch for $14.95 at Sartor Hamann's jewelry store.

Perhaps because he knew struggle longer than most who have found great achievement, and perhaps because he does not yet realize how capable he really is, Devaney handles his popularity with a kind of droll gingerliness, as if it were forged in smoke by a skywriter and subject to the first alien breeze. He has said that Nebraska fans are "understanding in defeat, but I would not want to put them to a serious test."

His personal panoply has improved immeasurably over the years (Willy Loman is now a fashion plate in smart checks and matching colors), but otherwise he has resisted any form of pretension. His telephone numbers are in the book. With the exception of the Nebraska-red drapes, red carpeting, red desk, red sheepskin rug, etc., his office is unspectacular, homey rather than huge, and the door is open to a casual flow of traffic — secretaries, assistant coaches, players in for a chat. On the wall directly below the prized No. 1 plaque from President Nixon is a carton of two derelicts sitting on a sidewalk, commiserating over their fate. One bum is saying to the other, "Then we lost our sixth game to Keen State. . . ."

Devaney still lives in a smallish, modestly appointed home on an elm-lined middle-class street in Lincoln, not yielding to the pressures (and the entreaties of Phyllis Devaney) to build something grand. And of an evening when he takes up his glass of milk and bourbon, that peculiar combination of aged license and scrupulous youth that somehow typifies him, takes it there in his basement den where Phyllis has tastefully assembled his crowd of trophies, the chances are he would rather talk about the days when he made $35 every two weeks doing "nonscientific" piecework in a Chevrolet foundry. Or about his grandfather, the tugboat captain. Or his Irish father (the name is De-*van*-ey, not De-*vane*-y) who worked the ore boats on the Great Lakes and wasn't home much. Or the time he tried boxing and "got whopped enough to realize it was not going to be my life's work." Or the time Phyllis wrote the term paper for him when they were at Alma College, and she got a C in the course and he got a B.

And when he finally gets around to analyzing his progress he will say that "situations trigger success," that coaches are lucky to hit fields that are ripe for seed, how this happened to lucky Bob Devaney at Alpena and Laramie and Lincoln. "I've worked hard. I've had my share of the dry heaves on Saturday morning. But I have been at the right place at the right time," he says.

This is a tidy oversimplification, of course. Football is a coach's game. Many coaches get good material; most coaches work long hours. A few are iconoclasts who contribute to the science of the sport, but not even these are assured winning records. The thing that separates the Devaneys (and the Bryants, McKays, Royals, *et al.*) from the journeyman of the trade is a gift they cannot alter much if they have it, cannot seem to acquire if they don't, and usually can't define or explain even to themselves. But Pepper Rodgers describes Devaney as "a man I would like even if he weren't a coach," and this is how he explains the gift:

"To be a successful coach, what do you have to have? A good staff, with good morale, that's first. Most of Devaney's assistants have been with him since he was at Wyoming. He pays them good. He relies on them. (Rodgers did not say it, but when Devaney was offered the head coaching job at Miami in 1963 he did a remarkable thing — he put it to a vote of his assistants. They voted to stay at Nebraska.) Head coaches don't coach much on the field anymore, so you've got to have guys who are loyal and won't watch the clock. Next you have to have a good athletic director. *He's* the athletic director. He's a good one.

"And then, then you've got to have a rapport with players. That's the key to the whole thing. You can have the best players in the world and lose if they won't play for you. It's like the dog food salesman.

His boss says, 'We've got the best dog food on the market, right?' 'Right.' 'And the best salesmen, right?' 'Right.' 'Well, how come we don't sell more dog food?' The salesman says, 'Well, I guess it's because the damn dogs won't eat it.' At Nebraska, the good players play for Devaney."

Bob Devaney coaching players, and players responding, is the stuff cocktail hours are hung on in Lincoln. A favorite involves Bob Brown, the All-Pro tackle who was on Devaney's 1962 and 1963 teams. Brown had a reputation for malingering. He made crises out of minor bruises. He missed practices. Finally, in the spring, Devaney picked up his uniform, and Brown came to his office to find out why. Devaney, deadpan, told him the coaches had decided that Brown should give up contact sports. "We recommend golf, or maybe tennis, where you can use your strength without getting hurt." Brown was 6-foot-4, 269 pounds. He cried for reinstatement. That fall Brown made All-Big Eight and the next year all-America.

Devaney does not lay down hard rules of deportment for his athletes, rules that would back him into corners. Coaches who have done that lately, he says, "are coaches who wound up losing face or losing their job." He does not try to regulate dress or hair, but the athlete who persists in being shaggy is fair game for the well-honed, and highly effective, Devaney needle.

It was not publicized, but a group of his black athletes came to Devaney with a "suggestion" list a couple years ago. Devaney has a reputation for being color-blind — he stacks blacks at a position if they are best at that position, but he is just as liable to mix the batter. He alternated his two tailbacks last year, and both were stars and one was black (Joe Orduna) and one was white (Jeff Kinney). Orduna is married to a white girl. Devaney says they make a fine-looking couple. One of his coaches, Bill (Thunder) Thornton, is black. Thornton played for Devaney.

The black caucus found it had nothing to argue about. When it was suggested blacks be assigned roommates by position, Devaney said fine. After a while the blacks asked if they could choose their own roommates. Devaney does not let small bones catch in his throat. He said that was O.K., too. When it was suggested that he made Orduna carry the ball too much, wearing him out, Devaney said, "All right, I won't have Joe carry the ball so much anymore." Orduna came to him privately. "Coach, I like to carry the ball," he said. Problem solved.

Vince Gibson says there "isn't a phony bone in Bob Devaney's body," and that this communicates to his players. They become willing subjects for his coaching impulses. For three years now the quarterbacking at Nebraska has been a cooperative venture between Jerry Tagge and Van Brownson. No complaints. "You don't know how tough coaching is until you've tried something like that and gotten away with it," says Gibson.

Boiled down, Devaney's ability with players would seem to be a matter of caring. He cares that his athletes graduate, and 75 percent do, an impressive number. He has been known to put lesser lights on traveling rosters just because the game was being played in their hometown. "You would absolutely die for Coach Devaney," says one former player, recalling a "moving experience" at a luncheon before the Sun Bowl game in El Paso, Tex., when Devaney was introduced and received a three-minute standing ovation — from his own players.

No real romance is complete without spats, of course. Devaney has been known to suspend recalcitrants — kick them off the team, deprive them of bowl trips — but he has a revivalist's zeal for the redeeming power of football and he holds to the doctrine of the second chance. Ironically, this gets him in the soup when it appears his humanitarianism may be self-serving. He refused recently to yield to pressure from some quarters that he banish star flankerback Johnny Rodgers, the team's leading pass catcher and kick returner who had been involved in a gas station holdup in May of 1970. In court, Rodgers received two year's probation. A student faculty committee took no action. Devaney deliberated, then also put Rodgers on probation, leaving him free to play this year. Reaction was mixed; there were some snickers in Missouri. Privately, Devaney said it would have been much simpler if Rodgers had been a fourth-team scrub. Then he would have given him his second chance and dismissed the case.

Because Devaney does not seem to take himself too seriously is not to say that he does not take himself seriously enough. He is a man of firm opinions, firmly held. He went before the Nebraska Unicameral last session at its request to speak for a new fieldhouse, and now Nebraska cigarette smokers are paying 5 cents a pack more in order for the school to get one. He does not back away from fights. He is at a standing simmer these days over a former Omaha sports editor who, after the 1969 season, polled Nebraska players on their choice for his successor. ("Who the hell says I'm retiring?" Devaney wanted to know.) In the Coaches All-American Game at Lubbock, Tex., this June (1971), he got into a shouting match with a younger, burlier game official who, Devaney felt, was blind to some unnecessary roughness. Bad words multiplied and for one appalling moment it appeared that a national television audience was going to see a fist fight between a respected college coach and a game official. Tempers cooled. The next day a friend said, "Hey, Bob, I didn't know you were that tough." "I'm not," said Devaney. "I was just bluffing."

Other coaches admire Devaney, says Rodgers, "because he stands up for the game. He says what everybody else wishes they had the guts to say." Devaney is an outspoken opponent of the N.C.A.A.'s 1.6 rule (eligibility for incoming scholarship athletes based on a projected grade average of 1.6). He feels it is not a true barometer for a kid who may develop late, especially hurting the black athletes. He is even less enthusiastic about proposed legislation that would limit scholarships to "need." The worms in that one, he says, are too numerous to count.

"How will you prove financial need? You will have to get personal financial statements from parents who won't want to give them. You'll have to use a cost-of-living index for every part of the country. A man making $15,000 in Fayetteville, Ark., can afford a lot more in life than a man making $15,000 in downtown Manhattan. What if you give a dentist's son a scholarship? Maybe the dentist hasn't pulled many teeth lately. But coaches will holler. They'll be at each other's throats."

What criteria, then, would Devaney use for aid?

Big smile. "That the boy be a good football player." Pause. Then, "And that he be in the upper two-thirds of his graduating class, or can pass an entrance exam. That's all. Simple as that."

There is no such thing as a "typical Devaney team." Like most good coaches, he adjusts to the available talent. At Wyoming his teams were quick and exciting; his early Nebraska teams were characterized by thick necks and slow feet. Twice embarrassed by smaller, faster Alabama teams in bowl games, Devaney himself began to sacrifice size for speed, and suffered through two mediocre years (6-4 in both 1967 and '68). Lately he has had size and speed, and a high-percentage passing game the concept and execution of which amazes Gibson. Nebraska completed 61 percent of its passes in 1970.

"Unbelievable," says Gibson. "No wonder I can't sleep."

Pepper Rodgers depicts Devaney as a "positive kind of coach," a man unafraid to take a chance. "Our third year at Kansas we had Nebraska by three points, two minutes to play, and Nebraska with fourth down and 13 on its own 20, or thereabouts. Most coaches would have punted and hoped for a break. Not Devaney. Tagge ran all around and finally threw an incomplete pass. Interference was called and we got an additional 15-yard penalty for protesting, and when it was over they had a first down on our 12. They scored. And we lost."

It is unlikely that Bob Devaney's Nebraska team for 1971 will be any more accommodating than it was as a national champion in 1970 — a big, fast, well-balanced team with a strong will to defend ground won. Devaney does not mind talking about these possibilities in the privacy of his den, surrounded by all those replica "1's," but his interest will wane and then he is likely to lapse into a whimsical recollection of those bowl games with Alabama and how Bear Bryant, after winning the first one 39-28 in Miami (in 1965), had called the next year and said, "Let's get together and have some more fun, Bob." And how Bob agreed, and they got together in New Orleans, and Alabama won, 34-7. And how a couple years later (in 1969) Bryant called again, suggesting they get together once more.

"I said, 'Which bowl did you have in mind, Bear?' and he said, 'Well, we were thinking about the Liberty Bowl.' I said, 'Gee, sounds great.' The next day we signed to go to the Sun Bowl."

But for pure Devaney, the gem was collected by John McKay of U.S.C. one year when McKay's team was playing in Lincoln. In the first half, U.S.C. was penalized four times for pass interference. Though ahead, McKay was livid. Muttering to himself as the teams broke for the dressing rooms, McKay suddenly found himself side by side with Devaney. He says Devaney grinned, rather sheepishly he felt, and said, "Well, John, how do you like my brother's officiating?"

THE 1971
COLORADO GAME

47

Nebraska Crushes Colorado For Win No. 18

By NEIL AMDUR
Special to The New York Times

LINCOLN, Neb., October 30, 1971 — The great debate continued today as Nebraska smothered Colorado, 31-7, for its 18th consecutive victory.

A few blocks from the hotel balcony where Nebraska's famous orator, William Jennings Bryan, had stirred crowds, the Cornhuskers offered persuasive credentials in college football's guessing game over which was No. 1 — Nebraska or Oklahoma.

Colorado was the first common foe this season. Oklahoma, which smashed Iowa State today to remain undefeated, whipped the Buffaloes, 45-17, two weeks ago.

Unless injuries or upsets sidetrack the two teams, their Thanksgiving Day showdown should be the game of the year.

Nebraska scored 24 points in the first half, then let its defense show off by stopping three Colorado thrusts to the Cornhusker 27, 20 and 24-yard lines in the last two quarters.

Nebraska's offense was directed efficiently by Jerry Tagge, a 6-foot-2-inch, 215-pound senior and pro prospect at quarterback.

Tagge passed 5 yards for one touchdown, scored on a 1-yard sneak and helped amass 324 yards on offense against a determined Colorado defense that showed the physical effects of countless injuries.

For those who believe in statistical comparisons, the Oklahoma machine accumulated 670 yards against the Buffs. On defense, however, the Cornhuskers allowed Colorado only 160 yards, less than half the total yielded by Oklahoma. Colorado had beaten Louisiana State and Ohio State and had lost only to the Sooners in seven previous games.

The Buffs' lone touchdown was only the second scored in the first half against the Cornhusker defense in eight games. It came on a broken pattern, when Ken Johnson, the sophomore quarterback, rolled out to his left, ran through the pocket under a heavy rush and found Cliff Branch behind a Nebraska defender for a 34-yard completion.

Two fumbles, however, one by Branch on a punt, and an interception were all the turnovers Nebraska needed in the half.

About the only deficiencies in the Nebraska repertory showed up in its kicking game. But Oklahoma's speed on offense was expected to pose considerably more problems for the big, strong Cornhusker linemen than Colorado did.

Nebraska appeared more emotional than usual in the first half en route to a 24-7 lead. Cornhusker players admitted before the game that Colorado carried special significance.

"They took some cheap shots at some of our guys last year," said Larry Jacobson, a standout defensive tackle, whose size (6-foot-6 and 250 pounds) belied a mild demeanor off the field. "We felt we owed them something."

Nebraskans are passionate about their team, because college football is the only game around. Despite a steady morning rain, 38-degree temperatures, brisk 20-mile wind gusts and the opportunity to watch the nationally televised contest in the heated comfort of a local bar or hotel, a crowd of 66,776 filled almost every seat in Memorial Stadium. Bright red raingear was everywhere.

Colorado helped the Cornhuskers open the scoring when Joe Duenas, its quarterback, fumbled the snap at his 10-yard line, and John Adkins, a Nebraska defender, fell on the ball.

Duenas, a 5-foot-7 sophomore, had been inserted to replace Johnson, who had run the first two offensive series smoothly.

Ever the opportunist in the tradition of great teams, Nebraska needed only two plays to score. Jeff Kinney burst 11 yards over right tackle for the touchdown.

A pass interception by Dave Mason, his fifth of the season, positioned Nebraska for a 65-yard scoring drive into the second quarter.

Tagge, who completed nine of 13 passes for 139 yards in the opening half, threw 30 yards into the wind to Johnny Rodgers, then 5 yards for the score to Maury Damkroger, which prompted a barrage of oranges from Nebraska rooters in the end zone. The Huskers have another Orange Bowl trip in mind.

But the Buffs refused to concede and moved to a touchdown with

160

10:04 left in the half on a 34-yard pass play from Johnson to Cliff Branch, the sprinter, who outraced Bill Kosch, the Nebraska safety.

SCORE BY PERIODS

Nebraska 7	17	7	0	—	31
Colorado...................0	7	0	0	—	7

48

Somebody Is Going To Be The Turkey

By DAN JENKINS
Sports Illustrated

NEW YORK, November 8, 1971 — A Colorado man sat in the cold, the wind, the rain and the gloom of Lincoln, Neb., last week and pondered whether he would rather die slowly of strangulation or have a dagger plunged into his stomach. These are the alternatives, said Colorado's assistant athletic director, Fred Casotti, if a football team has to choose between Nebraska and Oklahoma as an opponent. "They both kill you with a lot of pain," Casotti said. "It just depends on which kind of pain you prefer — fast or slow."

When the bruising, efficient Cornhuskers had finally finished destroying Colorado by 31-7, Casotti stood up from his seat and said, "Well, now I've got to go back to Boulder and get ready to answer seven thousand questions about Nebraska and Oklahoma and who we think is the better. I still don't know. But I hope the Nebraska defense doesn't line up on the runway at the airport in front of our DC-9. We'll never get home."

After these weeks of the 1971 season, Colorado, a common opponent, presented the first opportunity to compare Nebraska, voted the nation's No. 1 team, and Oklahoma, No. 2. Colorado had lost to O.U. 45-17, and Nebraska Coach Bob Devaney admitted before last week's contest that this would be the Cornhuskers' first "emotional" game.

Wandering around Lincoln on Thursday night with a couple of journalists, and while stopping in at a couple of saloons to visit with friends, the easygoing Devaney said, "I just hope we can get down to that game with Oklahoma on Thanksgiving in good shape. It ought to be something worth seeing. But I'm worried about Colorado. We don't know how good we are."

If he really didn't know it already, Devaney found out two days later that his 1971 team was probably the best he has had, among a lot of good ones. Nebraska simply manhandled Colorado in its usual physical way with perhaps a little more spirit and enthusiasm than the big sod busters normally display.

There had been a warning that something like this might happen on Friday as the Nebraska players moved out of the wind and drizzle into the dining quarters for their lunch of cold cuts and salad. Huge brooding types with relatively short hair who like to wear their letter jackets, the Cornhuskers, hidden out there on the plain where the wind blows from Laramie to Lincoln — untouched — sort of bristled at the mention of Colorado. And then Oklahoma, in that order.

"Colorado took some cheap shots last year," said Dick Rupert, a fine guard. "We kind of remember that."

Larry Jacobson, who might be an all-America defensive tackle despite his boyish grin and horned-rimmed glasses, said, "Naturally, we think about Oklahoma now and then. But there's no doubt in our minds that we'll beat them. There just isn't."

Quarterback Jerry Tagge talked about Nebraska's nonstar system and how it does not bother anybody, especially him, the prime mover of the team.

"It's almost become a tradition under Coach Devaney that we don't have any stars on the team," smiled Tagge. "We just have a lot of good football players who concentrate and carry out their assignments."

Tagge said, "It's funny. We don't all pal around with each other much. We have married guys and fraternity guys and we live all over town. My roommate isn't on the team. We see each other mostly at practice and then we go off to do other things. I think our success can be attributed to the fact that we just have a lot of good players and good coaches and great fans.

"You know, as a kid you dream about playing on a national championship team. Now here we are, this bunch of clowns you see around the room."

The Colorado game was never actually close because Nebraska did what it does best — make the enemy look bad. The defense provided a couple of fumbles at Colorado's 16 and 25, and these errors were turned into touchdowns. And the offense proved it could run and throw with a marvelous balance on two beautiful drives in the first half of 65 and 75 yards, which put the game out of Colorado's reach.

Unlike Oklahoma, which stays exclusively with the Wishbone T,

Nebraska shows the opponent a variety of offensive sets out of Devaney's I formation. Tagge, who has finally shaken Van Brownson as a compatriot quarterback and clearly has held the job all season, calls most of the plays himself, and expertly.

Against Colorado, he seemed always to know what would work, whether it was running his I-back, Jeff Kinney, over Rupert's left guard spot, or throwing to his ends and backs when least expected.

"The thing about Jerry," said Rupert, "is that he listens to you. He trusts you in the huddle to tell what might work. If I give him a nod, he knows I'm handling my guy and he can run there."

Tagge's leadership and certainly his passing arm are very much the key to Nebraska's success. He hit 10 of 17 for 144 yards and a touchdown on Colorado, and he had at least three perfect tosses dropped by usually dependable receivers such as the swift Johnny Rodgers and Jeff Kinney. His percentage is way up there — .615 — and he has thrown only two interceptions in eight games. No other quarterback who has averaged 10 completions or more a game can match these figures.

"We think our balance is just as impressive as Oklahoma's rushing," said Jacobson, the tackle. "They might gain 700 yards but they give up 500. We don't give up much, and I think our offense might be able to keep the football moving against them. I hope it can, anyhow."

Statistically, it will surely seem as if blazing Oklahoma has won the first comparison of the two top teams now that Nebraska has also whipped Colorado. Against a Colorado team that was in far better health than it was against the Cornhuskers, the Sooners outcomputerized Nebraska in every department, despite losing five fumbles.

Oklahoma rushed for 498 yards on Colorado while Nebraska rushed for only 180. And even though Tagge passed for 144 yards, Oklahoma's Jack Mildren chose that day a few weeks ago to hit three of four passes for 152 yards and two touchdowns.

"But this is misleading," Fred Casotti pointed out. "Nebraska had better field position because of its defense. It did what it had to do to win just as easily, like Devaney teams always do. And Nebraska sure bruised us more."

The Colorado players, for their part, felt that Nebraska was a slightly better team than Oklahoma, simply on its balanced offense and superior defense. Colorado Coach Eddie Crowder, naturally, wouldn't say which he liked better.

164

Casotti came close, however. "Nebraska is a lot more physical than Oklahoma. When they play on Thanksgiving Day, I figure Nebraska will dominate the game for 53 minutes. I don't know which 53, but for most of the day. But for those other seven minutes Oklahoma might score six touchdowns without Nebraska even touching them. But is six touchdowns enough? Who knows?"

Both Nebraska and Oklahoma have two more Big Eight games before they get down to each other in what will certainly be a thrilling day in the history of Norman, Okla., and maybe even the rest of the football-conscious country.

Nebraska has to play Iowa State and Kansas State, and Oklahoma must face Missouri and Kansas. None of these teams figures to do anything more than help the speedy Sooners and the growling Cornhuskers improve on their statistics.

Last week, Devaney brought up an item or two about the Oklahoma game that should give all those red-clad Cornhuskers a reason for some serious worry, even though the whole state is painted red and No. 1 signs are practically in the wash basins.

"People forget that we played a heck of a game last year," Devaney said. "It was 28-21, here in Lincoln, and they didn't know that Wishbone near as well as they do now. Also we didn't see much of Greg Pruitt. Now we have to go to Norman and they'll have all the folks in the stadium. I know they're better than last year. That's obvious. But I think we are, too. That's our hope."

So they move on. And the anticipation continues. And if an injury beforehand to some key player — Tagge or Mildren, Rodgers or Pruitt, for example — doesn't spoil things, Nebraska and Oklahoma on November 25 may collide in that most classic of football duels: speed versus power, big plays versus ball control.

Football brains say speed usually wins. But they say defense usually wins as well. Oh, well. Ho hum. Another game of the decade, folks.

THE GAME OF
THE CENTURY

49

This Year's Game
Of The Decade

By DAN JENKINS
Sports Illustrated

NEW YORK, November 22, 1971 — In college football there is this thing called the Game of the Decade and it always seems to be lurking in the doorway, like a Nebraska Cornhusker in a funny red hat or an Oklahoma Sooner in a funny red vest. A Game of the Decade is a rather special kind of contest something on the order of a Crucial Showdown or a Battle of Giants or maybe even a Game of the Century. And no matter how often they play one, a Game of the Decade is a combination of all that is wonderful and insane about college football.

It develops slowly. It starts out with a couple of teams like Nebraska and Oklahoma beating everybody in sight by six or seven touchdowns early in the season. As a result — and this is an essential ingredient — the two teams are ranked high in the national polls, preferably first and second. Then around mid-October everybody realizes that Nebraska and Oklahoma are not going to lose a game until late in the year when they meet each other. In, of course, a Game of the Decade.

As far as the 1971 supergame is concerned, it took a vastly surprising Oklahoma team to create the excitement. In early September it was obvious that Nebraska would hardly be exercised until Thanksgiving Day in Norman, when there would be this minor irritation, this remote possibility of an upset should the Sooners get high enough. That was fine, and Nebraska started off as expected — by burying everybody. Even Bob Devaney was moved to admit that his Cornhuskers might win a few.

While this was going on, though, Oklahoma was turning out to be more of a sprint relay team than a football team, and when the

Sooners ran circles around three excellent foes — U.S.C., Texas and Colorado — on successive Saturdays, it suddenly occurred to a lot of people that on November 25 there was going to be another Game of the Decade.

Now the two teams are there, as last week Nebraska bruised its way over Kansas State, 44-17, and Oklahoma sprinted past Kansas, 56-10. So, next week, get set for No. 1 Nebraska (10-0) against No. 2 Oklahoma (9-0) in still another of college football's gigantic, colossal, breathtaking, polldown Battle of Giants. Maybe even Game of the Century.

One of the most important things to understand about these Games is that they are sometimes more nerve-tingling before they get played than after they are over — when all of the players, coaches and fans, plus town, region and state of the winning school are stopping downtown traffic and when the losers are looking for a high ledge. Any old football-wise observer knows there is no more miserable creature in the world than a man whose team has lost a Game of the Decade, even on a fluke play, and at the same time there is nothing in the world more insufferable than a man whose team has won a Game of the Decade, even by pure theft.

As Darrell Royal of Texas once observed, "It's the fans who make it bigger than it is. For the players and coaches, it's just a big game. For some fans, it's something they might have to live with forever."

To be rather sticky about it, there are two different kinds of Games of the Decade. There is the mini-Game and there is the real Game. In the first a contest develops between a couple of teams that simply appear to be the best of the year, regardless of their records, teams that may have lost one or tied one along the way — as, for instance, the U.S.C.-U.C.L.A. happening of 1967.

The second kind is larger, and less frequent, but it has happened before. The teams involved should be undefeated and ranked No. 1 and 2, and they should meet late in the season. Which is to say that Nebraska and Oklahoma haven't invented anything. There have been many such classics, well remembered by historians.

The Nebraska-Oklahoma Game of the Decade seems to fall most comfortably into a category including these gems: Texas-Arkansas '69, Notre Dame-Michigan State '66, Notre Dame-Army '46 (which in some ways is in a class all by itself), Michigan-Minnesota '40 and T.C.U.-S.M.U. '35, games that were colorfully known, in order, as

The Big Shoot-out, The Game of the Year, The Game of the Century, The Battle of Giants and The Aerial Circus.

History tells us a few things we might expect from Nebraska and Oklahoma. For instance, it is a good bet that the game will be exciting, full of suspense. The home field seems to mean little, since visitors have won as many Games of the Decade as they have lost. Nor does being a favorite mean much, since the underdog has won half the time. The most revealing fact of all is that the team most reliant on the forward pass tends to lose. This could be taken as a bad omen for Nebraska. But it is also true that the team that wins the biggie usually does it with the aid of a pass — somewhere, somehow.

It emerges that the average number of Games of the Decade in, alas, a decade is four. Roughly every other season one comes along, one with the necessary ingredients of a long and proper buildup, unbeaten opponents, a national honor at stake and, when possible, some glamorous stars, if not an O.J. Simpson or a Bubba Smith or a Tom Harmon or a Glenn Davis and Doc Blanchard, at least a Jerry Tagge, a Jack Mildren, a Greg Pruitt and a Johnny Rodgers.

The decade which produced the most big games between No. 1 and No. 2 teams was the 1960's. Virtually every season, in a bowl if nowhere else, a No. 1 met a No. 2, or at least a No. 3. But the best single season for Games of the Decade was 1935 when there were three that captured the fancy of everyone. First, at midseason, Notre Dame and Ohio State, undefeated and untied, met at Columbus, and the Irish won in the last minute, 18-13. A few weeks later Princeton and Dartmouth, undefeated and untied, met in a blizzard at Palmer Stadium, and the Tigers romped, 26-6.

With these two Games of the Decade out of the way, the nation turned to a new area which was struggling for attention, the Southwest. Thus, on November 30, a week after Princeton-Dartmouth, 40,000 converged on a 24,000-seat stadium in Fort Worth for a T.C.U.-S.M.U. encounter that would decide the Rose Bowl invitation and the winner of The Knute Rockne Trophy for the national championship.

All of the world's leading football authorities, including Grantland Rice, were present that day in a bewildered Texas city to get bewildered themselves by a fellow named Sam Baugh, who threw 43 passes, an unheard-of number in those days. S.M.U. won, despite Baugh, in a 20-14 classic decided on a sensational pass play, while people drove their automobiles through wire fences in order to get near the field.

These days, happily, such measures are necessary in order for even 40 million people to watch a Game of the Decade. Most of the games have been turning up on television, and so will Nebraska-Oklahoma, at 2:50 E.S.T.

This particular Game of the Decade will match two teams as different as sprinters and weight lifters. Nebraska is a complete team, coupling a well-balanced attack with an iron defense. Oklahoma is all offense, most of it rushing out of the fashionable Wishbone T. Nebraska likes to probe and hammer, run and pass, work toward field position, and hold that line. Oklahoma only wants the football, and it will almost collapse that line in order to get it, the theory being that the Sooners will simply outscore you.

The statistics are telling on both sides. Devaney's Cornhuskers have allowed only 172 yards per game — best in the U.S. — a mere 6.4 points per game while offensing for 441 yards per game.

Meanwhile, Oklahoma has rushed for 481 yards per game, has a total offense of 563 yards per game and has scored 45 points per game — all tops in the country.

Nebraska thinks of itself as a team without stars, but stars have emerged. Jerry Tagge, the quarterback, is a star. He is big, strong, can pass to perfection, read defenses and lead. Johnny Rodgers is a game-breaker at running, catching and returning.

When Tagge passes and Rodgers catches, Nebraska can strike as quickly as Oklahoma does when Jack Mildren keeps the football or pitches it out to Greg Pruitt, Joe Wylie or Roy Bell on the triple option.

Both Tagge and Mildren are way up in there in total offense for the year, but they got there by different routes. Tagge has passed his way, Mildren has run, but each can do the other better than one might suspect. Interestingly, the touchdown ratio for each player is nearly equal. By throwing and running, Tagge and Mildren have accounted for 20 and 21 scores, respectively. And that's what counts. For all the fame of Auburn's Pat Sullivan and Washington's Sonny Sixkiller, Tagge and Mildren might be the two best college quarterbacks in the land. Certainly the most complete.

As for blazing Greg Pruitt's impressive rushing statistics (1,423 yards in nine games), Nebraska can counter with those of Jeff Kinney and Gary Dixon, who share the same position, Nebraska's I-back. Together they've gained 1,257 yards, most of it the hard way, but always churning forward. This means Nebraska runs, too.

In a sense, the game will match two different attitudes and systems, Nebraska representing the old, Oklahoma the new. In an era when the triple option and Wishbone are dominating the style of play, Nebraska has stuck with an I formation and all the variations Devaney can devise.

Oklahoma's Wishbone is more than the name, however. Coach Chuck Fairbanks, who installed it after last season began, has more speed than any team that has ever tried to play it. Pruitt is a streak, and so are Wylie and Bell. And Mildren is a player for whom the attack is perfect. He is a strong, fast, savvy operator who understands the offense. He reads the options and has the knack of being able to pitch the ball a greater distance — sometimes 20 yards, out to Pruitt — with more accuracy than any quarterback who has run it.

As both teams believe in their abilities to move the football, the question then is which team seems more capable of slowing down the other. Statistics would indicate that this edge belongs to Nebraska. But Oklahoma has played stronger teams outside the conference, like U.S.C. and Texas. So maybe the statistics are misleading.

Bringing it down to their five common opponents in the Big Eight, one can find edges for both. Oklahoma scored the more points, Nebraska showed the stiffer defense. They both won easily every week.

The one alarming figure in Oklahoma's disfavor — and one which surely gives hope to every Nebraskan — is the outrageous number of times Oklahoma has fumbled. The Sooners have managed to lose almost three fumbles per game. But without slowing down.

Can Oklahoma lose three fumbles and beat Nebraska? Probably not. But can Nebraska outscore an Oklahoma Wishbone that does not lose three fumbles? Probably not.

The answer to the enigma then lies in faster, more deceptive Oklahoma's ability to operate the most devastating attack in football today. Nobody really stops the triple option, because it has the enemy outnumbered. It stops itself. If the Sooners do not stop themselves, then they will win something that might be called — hey, gang, why not call it the Game of the Decade?

50

Sooners' Mildren
Predicts Victory

By NEIL AMDUR
Special to The New York Times

NORMAN, Okla., November 23, 1971 — The country and western music stations cry "Today's Teardrops are Tomorrow's Rainbows." Jack Mildren says, no sweat, Oklahoma's rainbow will be a victory over Nebraska here Thursday in their battle of unbeaten college football powers.

"I really think we're going to win," the blond Oklahoma quarterback said today, sipping a Coke at the Crossroads Restaurant, a campus hangout, while his attractive fiancee, Janis Butler, smiled admiringly. "Our whole team thinks so."

Mildren, a confident, poised senior who directs the country's most prolific offense, said, "Our coaches and fans are tighter than the players," over the nationally-televised Thanksgiving Day showdown of Big 8 Conference rivals.

Nebraska, the nation's No. 1 team and defending national champion, has a 10-0 won-lost record and a string of 20 consecutive victories. Oklahoma, No. 2 in all the polls, is 9-0.

Mildren, recruited from Abilene, Tex., has made Oklahoma's Wishbone series so effective this season that two newspapers in Nebraska devoted parts of their sports sections earlier this week to explanations of how it works and what the Cornhuskers must attempt to do to curtail the Sooners' efficiency and explosiveness. Nebraska is the nation's No. 1 defensive club, but has not faced a Wishbone or triple-option attack all season. "It's going to be people against people," said Mildren, a 6-foot, 195-pounder, who has lived up to expectations this fall as an option specialist after two frustrating seasons as a passer-runner. "Their defense has pride, our offense has pride in the Wishbone. I just think we've got the people."

Point-Prediction Made

Mildren already has told John Keith, the Oklahoma sports publicist, that the Sooners should score about 35 points against the Cornhuskers, who have not allowed more than 17 points in any game this season.

"Jack's amazing that way," Keith said, between handling the record number of writers, photographers and television personnel (totaling over 500) who have descended on this campus community. "Against Missouri, he knew that Missouri had a good defense against the Wishbone and he told me, 'Don't look for too much.'"

Oklahoma beat Missouri, 20-3, its lowest scoring output of the season.

Not since 1956, in the golden era of Bud Wilkinson, has a game so caught the fancy of Sooner fans, and for that matter, much of the Midwest and college football public.

The demand for tickets is so great that scalpers are asking and receiving $100 for a pair of $6 seats on the 45-yard line. The scalping situation prompted the student newspaper, *The Oklahoma Daily*, to query the Oklahoma City Office of the Internal Revenue Service whether the inflated prices charged by scalpers are in violation of Federal guidelines for the wage-price stabilization program.

The I.R.S. office, in turn, has queried Washington for a ruling.

"Even the fans are excited," Mildren said. "They'll come up and say, 'Hey Jack, good luck,' and all that. They're much more interested this week. They expected us to beat Missouri and the other teams. Against Nebraska, though, they're not sure. They don't know, so it's got them interested."

"We're ready," said Greg Pruitt, the Sooners' speedy halfback, who has predicted an Oklahoma victory. "I'm confident we'll win because I have confidence in our team and myself.

"I think we proved we played our best under pressure when we beat Southern Cal, Texas and Colorado in a row. I don't think Nebraska has played a pressure game this year."

51

Devaney Unveils A Wishbone 'Defense'

By NEIL AMDUR
Special to The New York Times

NORMAN, Okla., November 24, 1971 — Bob Devaney disclosed Nebraska's plans for defensing the celebrated "Wishbone" offense of Oklahoma tomorrow afternoon in their showdown game for college football's No. 1 spot.

"We're going to use the 'Pepper Rodgers Defense,'" the baldish Nebraska coach said today with a sly smile, after his Cornhuskers had finished a brisk, 30-minute workout in sunny 50-degree weather on the Tartan carpet at Owen Field.

The Pepper Rodgers Defense?

"Sure, you know, the defense that Kansas used to stop Penn State in an Orange Bowl a couple of years ago," Devaney continued.

"But Kansas had 12 men on the field," a writer reminded Devaney, a Big Eight Conference rival of Kansas.

"Now you got the idea," Devaney said, with a broad grin, eager to relax from the pre-game tension that has surrounded this meeting of the nation's top two teams.

Some Wish-ful Thinking

If Oklahoma's "Wishbone" offense is, as some observers have contended, indefensible, the Sugar Bowl-bound Sooners will be the No. 1 football team in the country after tomorrow afternoon's nationally televised game. The kickoff is 2:50 E.S.T.

But if the Cornhuskers, the nation's top defensive team as well as No. 1 in the polls, can solve the intricacies of the triple-option series, Nebraska's Thanksgiving Day wish could be the second straight national crown.

"There's a lot of people who say you can't stop the Wishbone,"

Devaney said, after watching Jerry Tagge, his fine quarterback, loosen up with passes to Johnny Rodgers, a favorite receiver, and one of numerous Nebraska threats on offense. "If you're a coach, you can't go along with that. You have to stop it."

Nebraska, unbeaten in 10 games, has yielded only 37 points all season. The Cornhuskers have had 10 days to study the Wishbone, which has made Oklahoma the most prolific running team in college football history.

Nebraska studied films of Missouri's fine defensive effort against the Sooners (Oklahoma won, 20-3, with its lowest point output of the season) and also last year's Cotton Bowl game between Notre Dame and Texas, another club in the Wishbone tradition. Notre Dame won, 24-11.

Chuck Fairbanks, the Oklahoma coach and a personal friend of Devaney, described the essence of the Wishbone as a "number ratio" designed to dictate as much responsibility as possible to the defense on both sides of the field.

The responsibility is based on the various options open to the quarterback in the triple-option series: (1) Keeping the ball and running or passing; (2) handing off to the fullback inside; (3) pitching out to a halfback. The name "Wishbone" is derived from the positioning of the backs in the shape of a wishbone as they line up in the backfield.

"The Wishbone's formation is a damn poor formation to line up in unless you can run it," said Fairbanks, who chucked previous power formations last year and was criticized for switching after an early-season loss to Texas last season.

A Joke, in Passing

Oklahoma can run the Wishbone, particularly Jack Mildren, the quarterback, and Greg Pruitt, a speedy halfback, who has averaged 9.5 yards per carry — helped by Mildren's adroit option pitchouts that sometimes resemble forward passes and confuse and successfully commit opposing defensive ends and backs.

"I think our quarterback is a hell of a passer," Fairbanks said teasingly. "He's just passing the ball backwards."

Devaney said Nebraska had not seen the Wishbone offense since last season, when the Cornhuskers beat Oklahoma, 28-21.

"But they've refined it so much since last year," the Cornhusker coach said, "that it's not even the same offense anymore. That's what makes it so tough."

Devaney said Nebraska "must control the ball" to thwart Oklahoma, which has averaged 45 points a game in nine victories.

"We better score about three or four times," he said, alluding to the possibility of a high-scoring game, although most crucial college football classics, of late, have been low-scoring games usually decided by defenses.

Fairbanks called Nebraska, "one of the most complete college teams ever assembled." Devaney, accepting the compliment graciously, said he would have to wait until January 2, following an Orange Bowl encounter with unbeaten Alabama, another nationally ranked power, before offering any further superlatives.

Nebraska, however, has not trailed in any game all season and has shown as much total offensive might as it has defense.

"I'll tell you this," Devaney said, "this is a very unusual game. Nobody's coming close to either team all year. You have to go back a long time in college football to find a game like this, with all of the various aspects so great."

52

Nebraska Rallies To Beat Oklahoma In Thriller

By NEIL AMDUR
Special to The New York Times

NORMAN, Okla., November 25, 1971 — Unbeaten, top-ranked Nebraska scored a touchdown in the final 98 seconds today to outlast Oklahoma, its national challenger, 35-31, in a college football classic that surpassed expectations for Thanksgiving Day excitement.

The Orange Bowl-bound Cornhuskers, who had never trailed through 10 previous victories, had to come from behind twice to register their 21st consecutive victory and 30th game without a loss.

It took a pressure-filled, 74-yard drive that consumed more than five minutes of the final period for Nebraska to regain the lead from the aroused Sooners, who also had trailed, by as many as 11 points, earlier in the game.

Jeff Kinney, a 6-foot-2-inch, 210-pound running back who seems destined for greater achievements as a professional, carried the last four times and 15 yards in the drive, including the final 2 for the decisive touchdown through a hole carved by Larry Rupert, the all-America guard.

Glover Finishes It

It was Kinney's fourth touchdown of the afternoon, and he finished with a shredded white jersey, 174 yards rushing in 30 bruising carries and totally "exhausted."

Oklahoma, with a 9-1 won-lost record and headed for the Sugar Bowl on New Year's Day against Auburn, had one final chance at its l9-yard line after the fifth Nebraska score.

But Nebraska made a strategic change in its defensive secondary and applied a hard rush on Jack Mildren, the Sooner quarterback.

On fourth down, Rich Glover, a junior middle guard from Jersey City, N.J., and a standout all day, rushed Mildren and deflected his attempt to throw long to Jon Harrison, his fleet wide receiver.

A record and raucous Owen Field crowd of 63,385 and an international television audience (the game was beamed by satellite to Europe and the Far East) had little time to let their midday holiday meals settle.

Johnny Rodgers, the Cornhuskers' explosive back, weaved 72 yards for a touchdown on a thrilling punt return after the Sooners' first offensive series. The furious pace continued for the entire game.

Almost No Foul Play

The two teams accounted for nine touchdowns and 829 yards total offense, including 311 in the first half by Oklahoma, which scored with five seconds left to take a 17-14 halftime lead on a 24-yard pass from Mildren to Harrison, his high school teammate from Abilene, Tex.

In a tribute to the consistency and quality of play throughout, only five yards in penalties were assessed against both schools.

Nebraska, the nation's No. 1 defensive team, spent 10 days trying to defense the various options and subtleties of the Oklahoma Wishbone offense. Yet Mildren, the 6-foot, 190-pound senior, was magnificent in defeat, running for touchdowns of 2 and 3 yards, throwing to Harrison behind a frustrated cornerback, Bill Kosch, for two more and amassing 267 yards total offense.

The Cornhuskers limited Greg Pruitt, Oklahoma's speedy all-America back, to his lowest output of the season, 53 yards in 10 carries. But Mildren's efficiency on the option and his ability to sustain long drives with crucial third-down calls reaffirmed the efficacy of the Sooners' attack.

Oklahoma scoring drives covered 70, 80, 78, 73 and 69 yards, and the Sooners averaged over 6 yards a play, incredible statistics against a team that had not yielded more than 17 points in a single game and had been called by Chuck Fairbanks, the Oklahoma coach, "one of the most complete college football teams ever assembled."

Nebraska has been termed "unemotional and efficient" in its tactical approach, and the two words summarized the Cornhuskers' comebacks, particularly on the last march.

Two Sooner fumbles led to Nebraska scores. But four Cornhusker touchdowns came on respectable marches of 54, 53 and 61 yards in addition to the winning 12-play drive after Harrison's second touchdown reception (17 yards) with 7:05 left had made it, 31-28, Oklahoma.

Twice on important third-down plays, Nebraska managed to avoid technical mistakes and maintain momentum. Kinney, who rushed for 154 yards in the second half, swept 17 yards on third-and-1 at the Cornhusker 35.

The biggest play of the game may have been Jerry Tagge's 11-yard pass to Rodgers on third-and-8 from the O.U. 46. Rodgers caught the ball lying on the ground.

"It's the greatest victory of my career," Coach Bob Devaney said afterward. "When we were down, 31-28, I thought we could score because our offense had been moving the ball in the second half."

In defeat Fairbanks acknowledged that it was a "classic game, the greatest one I've ever been involved in."

The Lost Chance

Oklahoma fans still thought the Sooners had a chance from the 19. But Devaney shifted Joe Blahak, the safety, to cornerback in place of Kosch, who had been victimized by Harrison for four catches and 115 yards.

In fairness to Kosch, it was the first time he had played cornerback in his varsity career. Normally a safety, he was shifted to play Harrison one-on-one in order to put Blahak, a strong tackler, closer to the Sooners' offensive muscle.

Mildren overthrew Harrison deep on first down, kept for 4 yards and was smothered by Larry Jacobson, a 250-pound all-America tackle, for an 8-yard loss before Glover, who was in on 22 tackles, batted the last ball away to send the Cornhuskers to the Orange Bowl with a chance for a second successive national title.

SCORE BY PERIODS

Nebraska 7	7	14	7	—	35
Oklahoma................3	14	7	7	—	31

53

Nebraska Rides High

By DAN JENKINS
Sports Illustrated

NEW YORK, December 6, 1971 — In the land of the pickup truck and cream gravy for breakfast, down where the wind can blow through the walls of a diner and into the grieving lyrics of a country song on a jukebox — down there in dirt-kicking Big Eight territory — they played a football game on Thanksgiving Day that was mainly for the quarterbacks on the field and for self-styled gridiron intellectuals everywhere. The spectacle itself was for everybody, of course, for all of those who had been waiting weeks for Nebraska to meet Oklahoma, or for all the guys with their big stomachs and bigger Stetsons, and for all the luscious coeds who danced through the afternoons drinking daiquiris out of paper cups. But the game of chess that was played with bodies, that was strictly for the cerebral types who will keep playing it into the ages and wondering whether it was the greatest collegiate football battle ever. Under the agonizing conditions that existed, it well may have been.

Quality is what the game had more of than anything else. There had been scads of games in the past with equal pressure and buildup. Games of the Decade or Poll Bowls or whatever you want to call them. Something played in a brimming-over stadium for limb, life and a national championship. But it is impossible to stir the pages of history and find one in which both teams performed so reputably for so long throughout the day.

In essence, what won it for Nebraska was a pearl of a punt return in the game's first 3½ minutes. Everything else balances out, more or less, even the precious few mistakes — Oklahoma's three fumbles against Nebraska's one, plus a costly Nebraska offside, the only penalty in the game. There was an unending fury of offense from both teams that simply overwhelmed the defenses, maniacal though they were. But that is the way it is with modern college football. You can't take away every weapon. Both Nebraska and Oklahoma stopped the things they feared most, but in so doing they gave up practically everything else. From Oklahoma's record-cracking Wishbone T, the Cornhuskers removed the wide pitch to the halfback, mainly Greg Pruitt, but in doing so they relinquished the keep, the fullback into the middle and most of all the pass. To stop Pruitt, the Cornhuskers were forced to cover wide receiver Jon Harrison man for man, which they did ineffectually, thus allowing Harrison to catch four passes in critical situations, including two for touchdowns. From Nebraska's imposing I spread and I slot, Oklahoma took away the passing game but gave up the power running attack. So the two teams swapped touchdowns evenly from scrimmage, four for four, and Oklahoma added a field goal. But always there lingered the one thing they had not traded, that sudden, shocking punt return by Nebraska's Johnny Rodgers.

It was one of those insanely thrilling things in which a single player, seized by the moment, twists, whirls, slips, holds his balance and, sprinting, makes it all the way to the goal line. Rodgers went 72 yards for the touchdown, one which keeps growing larger in the minds of all. And afterward, back on the Nebraska bench, he did what most everybody in Norman, Okla., probably felt like doing — he threw up.

"I don't know what I did or what I was thinking about," Rodgers said later. "The return was set up to the right, but I saw a hole to the left and cut back. I do remember seeing Joe Blahak up ahead and thinking he would get a block for me."

Oklahoma's Joe Wylie had punted the ball high and deep enough with the help of the gushing wind. The Sooner coverage was down fast, so fast that all of the 63,385 in Owen Stadium, not to mention the TV audience, must have felt Rodgers would have been much wiser to consider a fair catch. It never entered his mind.

Heavens to Omaha if Rodgers didn't catch it with Greg Pruitt right on him. He took the blow, spun around on his own 30-yard line and planted his left hand on the Tartan Turf to keep from falling. Strangely, Pruitt's lick only turned Rodgers away from the grasp of another lunging Oklahoma tackler, Ken Jones. With that, however, he set sail to the right. But just as quickly he then darted back to the left, through a whole cluster of wine-colored Sooner jerseys. There the minuet ended. Rodgers was open and away from the flow of the coverage that had developed, heading for the left sideline. Ahead, his friend, Joe Blahak, a cornerback, inherited the chore of screening off or blocking the last man with a chance to make a tackle, the punter, Joe Wylie.

Wylie never had a good enough angle on Rodgers, although Johnny (Rodgers) finally began to tire and Wylie is fast. It was academic; Blahak bumped Wylie, and from there on, Rodgers, who has been doing this sort of thing for two years — scoring on punts and making other big plays — could have crawled retching every inch and still scored.

What the punt return accomplished was monumental to the Nebraska cause. It ultimately allowed the Cornhuskers the luxury of an 11-point lead twice during the game, at 14-3 in the second quarter and at 28-17 late in the third quarter. It forced Oklahoma to go uphill all the way. And even when the Sooners' marvelous Jack Mildren overcame it twice, that bit of instinctive genius by Johnny Rodgers always had Nebraska's own brilliant quarterback, Jerry Tagge, in a position to retake the lead (or the game) with a single drive. Which Tagge coolly did when the scoreboard clock dictated that it was time, finally, and again, for the game to be won or lost by the Nebraska offense.

With 7:10 remaining in the fourth quarter, after Jack Mildren had run for two touchdowns and passed for two more to Harrison, his high school buddy from Abilene, Tex.; after Mildren — always, uphill — had Wishboned 467 yards in total offense for Oklahoma against the best defense in the country; indeed, after Jack Mildren had given the Sooners a 31-28 lead in a game that had every right, by now, certainly, to be running out of heroics, there was still Jerry Tagge, Johnny Rodgers, a refrigerator truck named Jeff Kinney and the Nebraska offense, which kept on coming like the disciplined Prussians they have become under Bob Devaney.

Devaney is normally a calm and likable man, resembling in that respect Oklahoma's Chuck Fairbanks. He had lost his cool only once during the game, he later admitted, when he turned to his defense on the sideline and said facetiously, "Why don't you guys give Rich Glover some help once in a while?" This was in reference to the fact that Glover, the nose guard, sometimes seemed to be stopping Oklahoma single-handedly. But when that last offensive drive of 74 yards had to be accomplished, Devaney was back in character. He was willing to let Tagge handle it. Devaney stayed calm. So did Tagge. So did they all.

The steady pounding had begun to wear down the Oklahoma defense, which had proved better than expected, and Tagge knew it. The ground game had worked throughout the second half, with Kinney banging his way to the 174 yards (and four touchdowns) he would eventually wind up with. The frenzied Oklahoma fans could sing "Boomer Sooner" and scream, "Defense, defense," all they wanted, but Jerry Tagge knew it had come down to his game to win.

"Nobody said a word in the huddle but me," Tagge said. " We all just knew what had to be done."

The drive required 12 plays and more than five minutes. Tagge would break out of the huddle and up to the line and frequently call an audible. He would key on the Oklahoma safety, who had to worry about a pass, and then run to the opposite side. He ran Kinney for a brutal 17 yards in which the big senior plainly broke three tackles. Tagge ran Kinney for 13 more yards on a play which saw the bruising I back cut grindingly outside and hammer down a wall of weary Sooners.

However, in between these two efforts by Kinney, whose white jersey was beginning to look like confetti, Tagge had to improvise a play that probably had more instant horror in it for both coaching staffs than any movie Vincent Price ever made. It was a pure shrieker.

Nebraska had come to third down and eight at the Oklahoma 46, trailing by three, the clock running, 4½ minutes left and the Sooners' Wishbone just waiting to get the ball one more time.

Now then, Jerry Tagge is not a fast man or very much of a scrambler, and while he is a splendid pro prospect because of his size and savvy, he does not have a quick release and he sometimes has trouble seeing any receiver other than the primary one — most often Johnny Rodgers.

Tagge called a pass right there, and the Oklahoma rush got him in quick trouble. He had no alternative but to run for his life, if not the ball game. He went out to the right, looking, looking, with O.U.'s best defensive end, Raymond Hamilton, closing in on him.

At the last second before being trapped for no more than a minimum gain, Tagge saw the squirming Rodgers between two Oklahoma linebackers. He drilled the ball low, but Rodgers sank to his knees and somehow caught it at the Sooner 35, just as he had somehow made that punt return. Enough for the first down. The Prussians were still coming.

Four plays and two minutes later it was second down at the Oklahoma six, and Tagge, who had been constantly glancing at the clock, called time-out. He knew that only a busted play could ruin Nebraska. Tagge wanted to chat with Devaney.

As Tagge remembers it, their conversation went something like this:

Tagge: "I know we can score, Coach, but I've been worried about eating up the time."

Devaney: "We're going for the touchdown. There won't be any ties."

Tagge: "We'll get it."

Devaney: "What's your best play?"

Tagge: "I think it's the off-tackle with Jeff (Kinney)."

Devaney: "O.K., let's run it without any mistakes."

Jerry Tagge and his friends did exactly that. Kinney slammed into the left side behind tackle Daryl White, knocked down somebody again and made 4 yards. So Tagge called the same play and Kinney rammed into the end zone. That, plus the extra point, made it 35-31 and sent an estimated 30,000 ecstatic residents of Lincoln, Neb., scurrying out to the airport to greet the football team that would keep all of the town's cocktail waitresses in their red sweatshirts with the white No. 1's on them until New Year's Day at least. And probably longer.

THE GAME OF
THE CENTURY II

54

Orange Bowl
A Classic Confrontation

By NEIL AMDUR
Special to The New York Times

MIAMI, December 31, 1971 — Bear Bryant is calling tomorrow night's Orange Bowl Classic "just about the biggest college game that's ever been," which is fine for Bryant: Alabama is No. 2 and its New Year's night opponent, Nebraska, is sitting in the hot seat.

Nebraska has been the No. 1 team in college football since last Jan. 1, when Notre Dame ended the long Texas winning streak in the Cotton Bowl, Stanford upset Ohio State at Pasadena, and the Cornhuskers rallied to outlast Louisiana State, 17-12, that same nervous night in the Orange Bowl.

Tomorrow night at 8 E.S.T., a capacity crowd of 76,000 and a prime time national television audience will see if Nebraska, as some rival coaches have claimed, is the "most complete college football team ever."

Nebraska, a 6-point favorite, has gone 31 games without a loss and has won its last 22 since tying Southern California, 21-21, early in the 1970 season.

A tie is the last verdict either team wants tomorrow. Since college football lacks a formal post-season championship playoff, Michigan could claim a national title with a Rose Bowl victory over Stanford and a Nebraska-Alabama standoff.

This 38th game has the quality ingredients to be billed a classic. Not since the 1955 Orange Bowl, when Oklahoma met Maryland, have two teams matched perfect records so late in the season.

En route to 12 victories this year, the Cornhuskers have outdistanced rivals by an average of 31 points a game, a feat unmatched by any of the great college teams in the past. The only school to score more than 17 points on the Nebraska defense, one of the country's finest, was Oklahoma, a 35-31 victim in their Thanksgiving Day thriller.

Alabama, once chided for its soft schedules during Bryant's successful national reign in the 1960's, has beaten five bowl teams this year and thwarted Southern Cal, 17-10, on the road in its opening game.

The Tide's turnabout from successive seasons of 6-5 and 6-5-1 has come from a well-balanced, mature defense and the installation and efficacy of the Wishbone offense.

"Last year, we held player meetings every Thursday night before a game," said Robin Parkhouse, a fine defensive end, and one of 'Bama's inspirational leaders. "We met for hours and didn't say anything. This year, we threw that stuff out, no pep meetings, just every player getting ready in his own way. . . ."

Nebraska seems to go about preparations with the technical efficiency of a professional team. Cornhusker players admit that getting as psychologically keen for this game as the season-long fanfare that preceded Oklahoma may be difficult to achieve.

"We're used to playing under pressure though," said Larry Jacobson, the 6-foot-5-inch, 255-pound all-America defensive tackle. "We've been No. 1 all season."

Bryant holds two earlier bowl victories over his colleague, Bob Devaney. All week Bryant has played the coy fox, as if another fresh trap was ready inside that familiar porkpie hat.

During a mid-week luncheon, Devaney recalled earlier pre-bowl musings with Bryant. The 'Bama coach would phone Devaney and say, "Old friend, let's get together in Miami and have a nice game." "I fell for it," the Cornhusker coach conceded.

Bryant is getting ready this week, too, and perhaps his confidence will rub off on his players. After Devaney rushed into a news conference from practice one day in a sweaty T-shirt, Bryant appeared resplendent in a $145 sport coat and trousers, the look of a man ready to move in.

The memory of the 39-28 Orange Bowl loss in 1966 and the 34-7 Sugar Bowl setback the following year may still haunt Devaney, who is college football's most successful coach.

55

Nebraska Crushes Crimson Tide In Orange Bowl To Earn National Title Again

By NEIL AMDUR
Special to The New York Times

MIAMI, January 1, 1972 — Exploding for three touchdowns in a four-minute burst during the first half, Nebraska crushed Alabama, 38-6, in the Orange Bowl tonight and confirmed its place as college football's No. 1 team for a second consecutive year.

The imposing Cornhuskers capitalized on a series of first-half errors and turnovers by their Southeastern Conference rivals and a 77-yard punt return by Johnny Rodgers to register their 23rd straight victory and 32nd without a loss.

The only question left unanswered by Nebraska's efficient, often awesome, display is whether the Cornhuskers are the most complete college football team ever. After impressive regular-season victories over Oklahoma and quality conference opposition, and again tonight against the nation's No. 2 team, who can deny them serious consideration?

Bryant Praises Victors

Bear Bryant, the Alabama coach, joined the list of beaten rivals who offered superlatives in Nebraska's behalf.

"I surely think they are one of the greatest, if not the greatest team, I've ever seen," said Bryant, whose career as a coach and player has spanned almost four decades. "They just toyed with us."

Offensively, Nebraska amassed more yardage and points in the first half, 225 and 28, than 'Bama had allowed per game in 11 previous triumphs.

Defensively, the Cornhuskers shut out the Tide when it counted, in the first half, and induced two fumbles, a high snap from center on a fourth-down punt and an interception that led to touchdowns.

4th Scoring Return

Rodgers showed the balance and breadth of Nebraska's striking power with his second-quarter run, his fourth scoring return of the season.

The most vivid example of the Cornhuskers' poise and power came after Terry Davis, the 'Bama quarterback, had scored the Tide's touchdown on a 3-yard fourth-down keeper round left end with 5 minutes 49 seconds left in the third quarter.

Refusing to give 'Bama an inch of momentum, Jerry Tagge, the fine Nebraska quarterback, and Jeff Kinney promptly moved Nebraska to five consecutive first downs that culminated in a 21-yard field goal by Rich Sanger.

The 76-yard drive consumed the remaining minutes of the quarter and culled whatever drama remained from the much-publicized national title game.

It also provided a satisfying moment for Coach Bob Devaney, college football's most successful coach, who had suffered successive losses to Alabama in major bowl games in 1966 and 1967.

A capacity crowd of 78,151 and a prime-time national television audience watched the first pairing of unbeaten teams in a bowl game since 1955.

But the aura of a "classic" was quickly diminished by the Cornhuskers, who won their first national title on the same field last year in a 17-12 Orange Bowl triumph over Louisiana State.

Alabama tried countless offensive maneuvers to disrupt the Nebraska defense. The Tide sent a running back wide out of its Wishbone formation and double-teamed Rich Glover, the Cornhuskers' all-America middle guard from Jersey City, N.J.

They even tried successive "flea-flicker" laterals on the last two plays of the first half that accounted for 32 of their 96-yard total offense in the half.

Nebraska, however, was simply too big, strong, and balanced for whatever magic Coach Paul (Bear) Bryant had planned in a bid for a fifth national championship.

Worst Loss for Bryant

The loss, in terms of margin of points, was the worst in Bryant's colorful and highly successful 14-year career at Alabama.

The only other Bryant-coached squad to lose by as much as 32 points came in 1954, during his first year at Texas A&M.

Texas Tech beat A&M, 41-9; Bryant won only one of 10 games that season. Nebraska's decisiveness over a 'Bama team that some observers were calling "Bryant's finest overall," was another tribute to the Cornhuskers.

'Bama finished with 290 yards rushing but an inability to mount any passing offense (Davis completed just 3 of 9 passes for 47 yards) kept the Tide from threatening Nebraska with the same balance that Oklahoma showed in defeat.

"In the first quarter, we took it out of them," said Glover, the 234-pound junior.

"We were so bad," said Johnny Musso, the 'Bama all-America running back, who tore up his No. 22 red jersey in disgust after the game. "They didn't force us into all those mistakes, we were just bad."

Devaney, who has been mentioned prominently for several head coaching positions in the National Football League, called the triumph "the biggest win of my career."

"The Oklahoma victory was a very important one to us," he continued. "We won the Big Eight championship with it. There probably was more excitement in that game because the lead changed hands several times. But this was for the national championship. I think I would have to vote for Oklahoma for the No. 2 team in the nation."

Heavy rain fell as late as an hour before the opening kickoff and cynics were suggesting that Bryant had ordered the showers to slow up the Cornhuskers' offense.

Alabama could have used a wet field in the first half. But the rain stopped 30 minutes later, and the synthetic playing surface absorbed the excess water well enough to avoid what might have been muddy conditions on natural turf.

In earlier bowl victories over Nebraska, 'Bama had surprised the Cornhuskers with speed and a deceptive passing game. But from the outset, as it did in 12 previous victories this season, Nebraska controlled the tempo.

SCORE BY PERIODS

Nebraska	14	14	3	7 —	38
Alabama	0	0	6	0 —	6

56

Bryant: Nebraska Toyed With Us

By UNITED PRESS INTERNATIONAL
The New York Times

MIAMI, January 1, 1972 — Paul (Bear) Bryant said tonight that Nebraska's Cornhuskers "toyed" with his Alabama football team and he shouldered the blame for the Crimson Tide's worst bowl beating.

"We were beaten soundly by a far superior football team. Their team was much better prepared than ours," a dejected Bryant said in the Alabama dressing room after Nebraska's 38-6 rout of the Tide in the Orange Bowl game.

"Actually, most of the time they just toyed with us," said Bryant. "They were one of the greatest, if not the greatest, I have ever seen.

"I feel like I had a real poor game plan," said Bryant without elaborating.

Not Mentally Down

"The people who played out there for us tonight won 11 straight games. I don't think they planned to go out there and get embarrassed and crushed, so I have to assume that it all happened because Nebraska was so great and I did such a poor job of getting us ready," said Bryant.

If he had it to do over again, Bryant said, "we would stick to our basic game and not try to do so many things — but I don't know what I would do to get us ready mentally." Bryant, however, would not say his team was mentally "down" for the game.

"We were just beaten by a great football team. . . . They just flat whipped our butts in every way known to man. We were never in the game."

The loss was the Crimson Tide's worst in 25 bowl games. It was also the first loss to Nebraska in three meetings of the teams — twice in the Orange Bowl and once in the Sugar Bowl.

Johnny Musso, the Tide's all-America running back, said, "everybody on offense played the lowest we've played all year — and I mean everybody. I'm not blaming anybody in particular.

"I think what happened was we just got tight and made all those mistakes in the first half. Heck, the offense gave 'em four or five touchdowns — we set 'em up and they scored. That's where we got beat."

'One of the Greatest'

Musso was sidelined in the final period with a pulled hamstring muscle in his left leg, but he said he had no problems with a previously injured big toe which had hobbled him during part of the regular season.

Nebraska, meanwhile, rejoiced at midfield of the Orange Bowl after locking up a second straight national championship.

"This is one of the greatest teams ever to play football," Nebraska's coach, Bob Devaney, said while toweling his chubby face after being thrown into the shower by his players.

Asked when he became convinced the Huskers were among the game's greatest teams, Devaney said, "Tonight."

The victory was Nebraska's 23d straight and extended its non-losing streak to 32.

"After ranking Nebraska No. 1," Devaney said when pressed about national rankings, "I would put Oklahoma No. 2 and maybe Colorado should be No. 3."

"The Big Eight is the toughest conference . . . no contest," said the game's star defensive lineman, Rich Glover. "Nebraska is, of course, on top with Oklahoma second and Colorado definitely third."

As for the beaten 'Bama team, Glover said, "I guess we hit a little too rough and a little too quick. As far as I'm concerned the pressure was off after we whipped Oklahoma, 35-31."

Green Carpet Unfolds

Johnny Rodgers, who broke a 77-yard punt return for a touchdown, said, "It started slowly, but then opened up and all I could see between me and the goal was that green carpet."

Devaney said the Orange Bowl triumph "was probably our most important victory ever, but the Oklahoma game on Thanksgiving had to be more exciting."

57

All Yours, Nebraska

By DAN JENKINS
Sports Illustrated

NEW YORK, January 10, 1972 — When there was a football game out there to be won, which was not very long, it was difficult to see anyone but those old familiar Nebraska heroes doing what few people except themselves and Bob Devaney knew was possible. Which was the modest stunt of taking Bear Bryant and Alabama and making them look like your neighborhood Texas A&M with a little dash of Oklahoma State thrown in. The 1972 Orange Bowl was the game of what decade? The 1950's before Bear got to Tuscaloosa? The only game going on for anyone to watch last Saturday night in Miami was between Nebraska's Johnny Rodgers and Rich Glover, to see which one of them could do the most to make it the worst thing that ever happened to Bear Bryant.

One has to look back and wonder what kind of odds a Nebraskan could have gotten from an Alabamian before the opening kickoff if the fellow had said he felt that his Cornhuskers would whip the Crimson Tide worse than Nebraska had whipped Oregon . . . Minnesota . . . Texas A&M . . . Oklahoma State . . . Colorado . . . and Kansas State? Or what if the Nebraskan had said what one of Bob Devaney's associates had whispered, with a sincere expression, that the score would be about 40-7, not knowing that the actual count of 38-6 would be enough to make it the worst loss of Bryant's Alabama career and equal to the worst of his entire life? A lot of people close to Devaney insinuated such madness, and Alabamians only thought them crazier than Miami Beach itself.

What makes this worth dwelling on is that Bear Bryant was in town as the coach with the reputation, the mystique, the image of the man who can, simply by being around, lend all the glamour and stature that any football situation or game ever needs. And Bob Devaney was there in his accustomed role of good old boy, a man who has never actually had it, despite his own brilliant coaching record.

Devaney has no real star quality, not outside of Nebraska, that is. At least not until right now, this very moment, which finds him and everybody from Nebraska giddy with the delights of a second straight national championship. Celestial fame has set in with the fact that when the Cornhuskers had to go up against all of the Alabama mystique, they calmly shrugged it aside and turned the whole affair into a joke by halftime.

It was 28-0 then. And Rich Glover had made himself as much a part of Alabama's backfield as, shall we say, Johnny Musso. And Johnny Rodgers had already made his usual punt return for a touchdown. And the Alabama Wishbone had been gnawed bare.

"As a matter of fact," said Rodgers later, "a few of us did talk a little bit at the half about the celebration party we were going to have back at the hotel."

While Nebraska got a couple of good breaks that demoralized Alabama early — a clear-cut interference call to set up the first touchdown and a head-ringing fumble to set up the third, both within the game's first 18 minutes — there was something else down there on the field that removed any doubt about the outcome. It was the fact that homebody Devaney had a far better game plan than Bryant — and far better athletes to run it.

The most impressive thing about Devaney's Nebraska teams is their discipline and balance. Normally, football teams that rely as much on the forward pass as the Cornhuskers do in their endless I-slot and I-spread formations have a tendency to become eventually nothing more that passing teams, and that won't cut it. Nebraska never has slipped into this fault. It can always run, as indeed it ran on Alabama, with Jeff Kinney and Bill Olds bruising their way for some killing yardage out of what were designed to look like throwing formations, which is what the game plan was all about.

Meanwhile, Alabama's offense was a sad sight. All season long its Wishbone had never looked quite right, despite the victories the Tide kept rolling up. It lacked deception and outside speed, and Alabama quarterback Terry Davis even confided to a friend before the Orange Bowl, "I've never had to throw when we were behind. I'm not that confident about my passing. I hope we don't get in that situation."

Alabama quickly did get in that situation, mainly because of the last play of the first quarter, when the incomparable Johnny Rodgers stabbed the Tide with a punt return just as he had mortally wounded Oklahoma with one. Once more, he made the biggest play in a big game.

Rodgers took this punt on a sudden bounce 77 yards from the Alabama goal, with red jerseys engulfing him. A swerve to the right, quickly, a turn upfield, a couple of blocks, an alley, and it was burn, baby, burn, right past the Alabama bench. Following a two-point conversion it was 14-0 and get the champagne ready.

"Johnny's return and a couple of good defensive plays stunned them," said Nebraska quarterback Jerry Tagge, who did his usual masterful job of passing and *reading*. "The thing was, we never really got to see what we could do against them, but everything was working."

The Nebraska coaches knew all along that it would.

"Their Wishbone is two years behind Oklahoma's," one of them said privately. "They must not believe in it totally themselves, because they go to other things at times. We could have beat them bad but Bob isn't that kind of guy."

Which is true. When Alabama's Davis went out with an injury early in the fourth quarter, Devaney took out Tagge, just to be sporting. The game was over, anyway.

One thing about The Bear, though. He's always equal to a loss.

"We were beaten soundly by a far superior team," he said. "I wouldn't have minded our bunch playing lousy if we could have lucked out and won. But they toyed with us most of the time. They might have been the greatest I've ever seen."

That theme, of course, was sounded before Saturday night ever arrived. Everybody is "great" and "proud" and "happy" to be on hand at every bowl game ever played. This one was so extra special there were two press conferences daily all week long, but they were hardly revealing. Either Bryant or Devaney would enter the little room off the driveway at the Regency Spa Hotel in Miami Beach and try to kill the other with lavish praise. And a man keeping count claimed Bryant and his assistants used the expression, "We're very proud to be here," between 60 and 100 times, a phrase they didn't get to use even once after the game.

Nor was it easy to get a line on the game by observing or chatting with the players on either team. As a group, the Alabama team seemed more noncommittal, more aloof, perhaps a bit more cocky. Not so much in what few things the players said, but simply in the way they walked, sat, grinned or didn't grin, in public.

Nebraska's players seemed noticeably more at ease than Nebraska's coaches, and there might have been a good reason: Bob Devaney.

"We've tried to see that they have fun, and I've tried not to impress on them the personal importance that I feel about this game," Devaney said. "I've lost twice to Bear and I don't like to think that there's a guy around who can just walk out on the field and beat me any time he wants to — even if his team is very good.

"Fortunately, these players of ours aren't as aware of the Alabama stigma as we coaches. They were only in high school somewhere when Bear beat us in the 60's."

Devaney lost two in a row to Bryant in Miami and New Orleans after the 1965 and 1966 seasons. It was the first one that hurt the most, for it meant another national championship in another era. Those losses (39-28 and 34-7) did very little for Devaney's image.

The fun the players had consisted of all the things that bring people to a city that would name a roadway after Arthur Godfrey. Both schools dressed their men up in their red blazers and sent them out nightly to shows at various hotels, some of the shows featuring singers and some featuring chorus cuties. They also wound up at the racetracks and the Seaquarium. Nebraska's team even managed to have a dinner at the Bonfire, one of the 79th Street Causeway's best restaurants for sporting types.

Except for one workout a day, which never seemed too harsh, the players had a good deal of time at their respective hotel pools to lie in the sun in tank shirts and shorts. For whatever it was worth, Devaney allowed the Cornhuskers to swim and play frivolous games in the pool. Bryant did not allow swimming. Just drowning, somebody said later, in tears.

There were no comics among the players, but some of them did struggle to convince everybody that they were not getting nervous or tense. Jerry Tagge mentioned at one point that "it's sort of tough to get up for a game in Miami." Jeff Kinney confessed that he had preferred basketball to football in high school. And Rich Glover, in reply to his thoughts about the Crimson Tide, said, "I'm just sitting by the pool listening to soul music on my radio."

It was left to Terry Davis to supply the week's only quality mirth. Asked what it was like to be the field general of a full-house back-field of wine makers, the reference being to Johnny Musso, Joe LaBue and Steve Bisceglia, Davis responded: "Sometimes it's con-fusing with all those foreigners there. While I'm calling signals, one of 'em will be asking the other one what the play is, and one of 'em will be asking another one what the snap count is. I should have majored in Italian."

Alabama deserved one laugh. And so ended the Orange Bowl laughter.

Thus the long day worked out just the way Larry Jacobson had said it would. Jacobson, the big Nebraska tackle, was lounging by the swimming pool one day last week, "Come Saturday night, there won't be anything else to discuss," he said. "We'll still be No. 1 and Oklahoma will be back to No. 2."

So it was. As a lot of people had known all along, the real Game of the Decade had already been played back in Norman, Okla., on Thanksgiving Day.

THE 1972
OKLAHOMA GAME

The Cornhuskers' vaunted defense snags Oklahoma quarterback Jack Mildren (11).

MALCOLM EMMONS

I-back Jeff Kinney (35) blasts through an opening in the Sooner defense in this epic contest.

In the 1972 Orange Bowl against Alabama, also known as Game of the Century II, Johnny Rodgers broke loose on another of his pattened long runs.

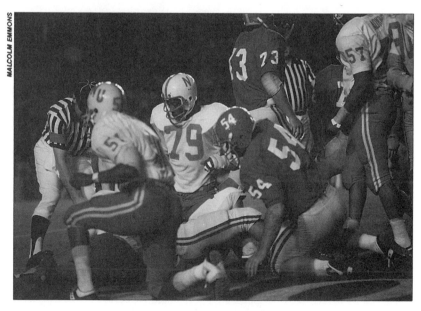

Rich Glover (79) and the remainder of the Nebraska defense kept Alabama bottled up the entire evening.

In the end, Bob Terrio and Bill Janssen (55) celebrated Nebraska's 38-6 victory over the Crimson Tide and their second national championship.

Johnny Rodgers hurdles a Kansas State would-be tackler in 1972 en route to winning
the Heisman Trophy.

Bob Devaney: a teacher, a leader and a winner.

58

Sooners Get Revenge Over Nebraska

By NEIL AMDUR
Special to The New York Times

LINCOLN, Neb., November 23, 1972 — Oklahoma stopped Nebraska's elusive roadrunner, Johnny Rodgers, and spoiled Coach Bob Devaney's going-away party with a 17-14 victory over the Cornhuskers today.

The once-beaten Sooners, headed for a now attractive Sugar Bowl date against Penn State on New Year's Eve in New Orleans, rallied from a 14-0 deficit in the second half and dealt the two-time defending national champions their second defeat in 11 games and their first setback in 24 games and in the "House That Bob Built," Memorial Stadium.

The 57-year-old Devaney, college football's most successful coach, will retire after the Cornhuskers' Orange Bowl meeting against Notre Dame on Jan. 1 in Miami to devote full time to his duties as athletic director, unless an attractive pro offer lures him from the collegiate ranks.

Field Goal Decides

Today's game, before a record crowd of 76,587, lacked the drama, quality and frantic pace of last year's 35-31 Thanksgiving Day classic in Norman, Okla., won by Nebraska But it was a satisfying reversal for the Sooners, beaten only by Colorado in 10 games, who now need a triumph over Oklahoma State on Dec. 2 to unseat Nebraska as Big 8 Conference champion.

The margin of victory was a 41-yard field goal by Rick Fulcher with 8 minutes 44 seconds left, after the Sooners recovered a Nebraska fumble at the Cornhusker 38-yard line.

But it was Oklahoma's ability to shift from its ground-oriented wishbone offense, mount a successful passing attack and control Rodgers, the controversial Heisman Memorial Trophy candidate, that produced what Coach Chuck Fairbanks later described as "one of the greatest victories of my coaching career."

The Sooners played almost the last three quarters without Greg Pruitt, their leading ground-gainer, who was nursing a tender right ankle and carried only twice during the game. They also lost their top receiver, John Carroll, in the second quarter and were forced to turn to a 17-year-old freshman, Tinker Owens, for crucial receptions that keyed two second-half scoring drives.

Owens, a 170-pound younger brother of Steve Owens, the former Oklahoma Heisman Trophy winner, caught passes of 38 and 13 yards from Dave Robertson in a 76-yard march that ended with a 2-yard scoring run by another freshman, Joe Washington.

Owens Sees Double

Nebraska tried to double-team Owens. But Owens, under order from coaches in the press box, split wider at the line of scrimmage to neutralize the double coverage and wound up with five receptions for 108 yards.

He outfaked Zaven Yaralian on a 20-yard sideline pass that moved the Sooners to the Cornhusker 10 early in the fourth quarter. Two plays later, Nebraska defenders were called for tripping Owens on a slant pattern over the middle, the ball was positioned at the l-yard line, and Grant Burget scored on the next play.

For much of the game, Nebraska fans seemed more concerned with selling Rodgers to a national television audience and embarrassing Coach Paul (Bear) Bryant of unbeaten Alabama for "chickening out" in selecting the Cotton Bowl over an Orange Bowl rematch against the Cornhuskers.

Rodgers, who returned a punt 72 yards for a score in last year's thriller and ranked third on the all time collegiate list for touchdown frequency, was stalked, often chided, and shut out today by Ken Pope, an aggressive 205-pound junior cornerback and Pruitt's roommate.

"I wanted to play a tough game because Pruitt's up for the Heisman Trophy, too," said Pope, who was named the game's top defensive player. "This inspired me, and I felt like I could cover Rodgers."

Rodgers gained only five yards in four carries, caught three passes for 41 yards and managed to return only one of nine Sooner punts for seven yards, well under his career average of 14 yards a play. The 173-pound senior wingback had one potential 43-yard touchdown pass play nullified late in the second quarter when he stepped out of bounds at the Oklahoma 28-yard line before catching the ball.

Nebraska took advantage of two fumbled punts for both its scores. The first touchdown, a 14-yard burst by Bill Olds, the fullback, gave the Cornhuskers a 7-0 lead at 7:32 of the opening quarter.

Another fumbled punt, one of four Sooner fumbles, gave Nebraska possession at the Oklahoma 14. The Cornhuskers scored in six plays with Dave Goeller diving across from the 1.

SCORE BY PERIODS

Oklahoma	0	0	7	10	—	17
Nebraska	7	0	7	0	—	14

59

Neither Rodgers Nor Pruitt Was Able To Do It

By PAT PUTNAM
Sports Illustrated

NEW YORK, December 9, 1972 — Here now is an easy game called name the Heisman Trophy candidates. Clue one: This fellow, call him Greg the Limp, played Thanksgiving Day and ran twice for seven yards. No, he did not catch a pass, return a punt or throw a block. For a bonus clue: His team gained only 141 yards on the ground and lost four fumbles. Nothing sounds familiar? Try this one: Call him Johnny the Ignored. In the same game he ran four times for five yards, caught three passes for 41 yards and ran back one punt for, ah, seven yards. And his team lost three fumbles, had three passes intercepted and gained 77 yards rushing. Last clue: Greg's team came from behind to win, 17-14, and the stars were Ken Pope and Tinker Owens. Tinker, T-i-n-k-e-r, as in Tinker Bell. What do you mean, sober up?

The way things have gone for Oklahoma and Nebraska this season, lack of success on Thanksgiving by Greg Pruitt and Johnny Rodgers should hardly have been surprising. Before the season began, it was said that this game would be for the national championship. But Nebraska came up three points short in its opener against U.C.L.A. and was lucky to escape with a tie against Iowa State. Oklahoma was dumped by Colorado and had to struggle to beat Missouri. Two weeks ago Pruitt, the speedy little Sooner senior, came out of the Kansas game with a badly twisted left ankle, and suddenly his chances for the Heisman Trophy depended not so much on how well he did against Nebraska but on how well Oklahoma did against Johnny Rodgers. "I'm going to try, but is doesn't look too good," Pruitt told his roommate, Ken Pope, the 205-pound junior cornerback who would be assigned to cover Rodgers. Pope laughed. "Don't worry, man. If you want the Heisman Trophy, I'll get it for you. I'll play that guy so tough he'll think I'm the number on his back."

"You better," said Pruitt, "because if you don't you won't have any place to sleep. Anyway, I've told you all along that if you room with a superstar, some of it is bound to rub off. Now you can prove it."

Pruitt said he wanted to start, and Oklahoma let him, but it was obvious from the beginning that the Big Eight Conference's second leading scorer (behind Rodgers) would not last long. "I was hurting something awful," Pruitt said. "I knew I could play the whole game if I was lucky and if I could avoid any contact, but I just couldn't figure how to do that." He carried the ball but twice, and in the second quarter he left the game for good. "Relax," Pope told him after he limped to the sideline. "I own Rodgers, and he knows it because I keep telling him."

"I hope so," said Pruitt, "because it's up to you to win." Pope discovered that he had to work less than he expected. Oddly, Nebraska almost ignored its 172-pound senior ace as it built a 14-0 lead midway through the third quarter. Both scores came after Oklahoma fumbled punts. In the first quarter, Rodgers carried twice on reverses for minus one yard, and of two passes thrown to him by sophomore quarterback Dave Humm, one was incomplete and the other, although complete, fell a yard short of a first down. The second quarter was only slightly more productive. Rodgers caught one pass for 20 yards, but with a 7-0 lead at halftime and Oklahoma playing like it had never seen a football before, it appeared that Nebraska really did not need him.

At halftime Chuck Fairbanks, the soft-spoken Oklahoma coach, tried to rally his troops in the dressing room. "We've made some mistakes, but so have they," he said. "All you can do is forget the first half and go out there and play like the score is tied." Then he asked if anyone had anything to say.

"Yes, sir," said Tinker Owens, a 17-year-old split end and the younger brother of Steve Owens, Oklahoma's 1969 Heisman Trophy winner. Tinker had gone into the game when John Carroll, a junior, was injured in the second quarter. "My man has been going for every fake and I've beaten him on every play." "We'll see," said Fairbanks. But Oklahoma opened the second half the way it had played the first, trying to establish the running attack that was tops in the nation. It didn't work. The Sooners fumbled away a second punt, and Nebraska went in to make it 14-0.

"Put the ball in the air," Fairbanks told quarterback Dave Robertson. "And don't forget Owens."

After Nebraska kicked off, Oklahoma started from its 24, and right away Robertson went to Owens. The first pass was broken up, but the second came down into the young freshman's hands, and it picked up 38 yards. Then Robertson went to his tight end, Al Chandler, for 16 yards and came back to Owens for 13 more. "Oh," said Nebraska, and shifted Monster Man Dave Mason over to help cover Owens. No matter. At the Husker 7-yard line, the Sooners went back to their ground game and, on the fourth run, freshman Joe Washington cruised around right end for a yard and a touchdown to make it 14-7.

Early in the fourth quarter, the Robertson-to-Owens combination put Oklahoma in gear again. Upstairs in the press box, Barry Switzer, Fairbanks' top assistant who calls all the Sooner plays from his lofty perch, phoned down to tell Owens to split out an extra 10 to 15 yards. The move nullified Mason, who could not afford to follow Owens that far from the action. Zip. Owens pulled in a 22-yard pass at the Nebraska 10. Two plays later, he was tripped as he went for a pass in the end zone, interference was called and Oklahoma had a first down at the one. Grant Burget, Pruitt's sub, carried in from there to tie the score.

A few minutes later, Oklahoma's Lucious Selmon recovered a Nebraska fumble at the Husker 27. Rick Fulcher made the most of the opportunity with a game-winning 41-yard field goal.

And Rodgers? Well, he ran twice more in the second half and he caught one more pass, and that was all. Of Oklahoma's nine punts, he tried to turn on his dazzling magic but once, and Oklahoma turned that off after only seven yards. But still, he had his moment, even if it didn't count. With the score 7-0 and the ball at the Oklahoma 43, Rodgers went streaking down the sideline, took a Humm pass at the 12 and slipped past a defender for an apparent score.

Not so, ruled Referee Vance Carlson. He pointed at a spot near the 39-yard line and said that was where Rodgers had stepped out on his way down the field to catch the pass.

"I stepped out," said Rodgers, "but that guy (and he pointed a finger at the grinning Pope) pushed me. I thought if I was pushed out, I could come back in."

"When you're out," said Carlson, "you're out."

"Too bad, Johnny," said Pope, still grinning. "That was a very nice catch."

Later, Pope admitted he had worked on Rodgers almost as much verbally as he had physically. "But nothing mean," he said. "Just things like, 'Nice block, Johnny' or 'Aw, Johnny, I thought you could block better than that.' But I don't know if it worked. He would just grin when I'd say something and go away. But I'll tell what did work. We really stuck it to him out there every chance we got. Stick and stick. Dan Ruster really stuck it to him once. He went up, and when he came down I thought he had broken his back. (Rodgers in fact did play the entire second half with two cracked ribs.) After a while he began hearing footsteps. He dropped one pass that was right into his hands, and I was still five yards away from him. I wonder if Greg will let me hold the Heisman Trophy sometimes?"

Rodgers was not even mildly upset by Pope's observations. "I don't hear footsteps," he said quietly. "The only thing wrong today was that Humm wasn't getting the ball to me on time. I don't think I was given the chance to do anything, so I don't see how that No. 28 (Pope) could think he did so well against me."

'What about the Heisman now?" he was asked. Rodgers' eyes went blank behind his shades. "I know darn well they aren't going to give it to anybody because he is a better football player than I am. They may not give me the trophy, but Johnny Rodgers will always know he won it."

THE HEISMAN

60

Moral Issue Haunts
Heisman Voters

By NEIL AMDUR
Special to The New York Times

LINCOLN, Neb., November 25, 1972 — With official ballots in the mail, a delicate moral question continues to haunt the final Heisman Memorial Trophy selections, already the source of increasing national debate.

The latest problem for college football's top individual award involves Johnny Rodgers, the all-purpose Nebraska back, and his series of run-ins with law enforcement officials.

A number of Heisman electors have said publicly and privately they will not vote for the 170-pound Rodgers because of an off-the-field background that includes a 1970 arrest for a gas station holdup that netted him $90. Rodgers, who was stopped for driving with a suspended license earlier this year, also has been the victim of numerous private jokes about his past, one of which led to a near-brawl at a local bar the night before yesterday's Oklahoma-Nebraska game.

"I still feel I'm the best athlete," the senior wingback from Omaha, Neb., said after a somewhat unspectacular showing in the Cornhuskers' 17-14 nationally televised loss to Oklahoma yesterday. "I don't see how persons in New York and California can say they know me. In 21 years I've had only one really bad experience.

"I can look back and see 10 or 12 other times I could have done something, and I didn't. I'm not ashamed of the way I am. I think I've done a pretty good job of raising myself."

Coincidentally, the publicized fuss over Rodgers may have squelched the Heisman hopes for college football's finest lineman, Rich Glover, Nebraska's two-time all-America middle guard from Jersey City, N.J. In a year with no outstanding backfield candidates like an O.J. Simpson or Jim Plunkett, Glover was considered a strong possibility to become the first lineman since Leon Hart to win the award. Being on the same team with Rodgers cannot help Glover's chances, though.

The Heisman balloting deadline was pushed back this year to include the last major weekend of the regular season, Dec. 2, undoubtedly in response to criticism of last year's selection before Thanksgiving Day. Pat Sullivan, a quarterback from Auburn, was the 1971 recipient.

As in previous years, sectionalism probably will govern the mood of many electors. At this time, the top candidates, listed alphabetically, would appear to be Glover, John Hufnagel (the Penn State quarterback), Bert Jones (the Louisiana State University quarterback), Greg Pruitt (the Oklahoma back) and Rodgers.

If Rodgers were to win the award, he would not be the first Heisman recipient whose background came under fire. Several previous winners had problem pasts that included flare-ups with local authorities.

Few electors surveyed for their views on the situation questioned Rodgers' credentials on the field, which include the third highest touchdown frequency of any college back in history and a 14-yard average per play. The debate appears over whether he should have been allowed to continue playing at Nebraska and whether moral values have any consideration for the Heisman Trophy, and if so, how much.

There have been other side effects in the dispute. Besides the private jokes, which evoke more response from intense Nebraskans than the Soviet wheat deal, Rodgers claimed earlier this week that local police authorities were hounding him at all hours at his apartment — a charge denied by the police department.

"You wouldn't have all this noise either, if Rodgers were white," one local bartender noted. "But because Johnny's black and because he's had a few problems, he gets blown up."

61

Rodgers Of Nebraska Voted Winner Of Heisman Trophy

By AL HARVIN
Special to The New York Times

NEW YORK, December 5, 1972 — After a heated controversy over whether his off-the-field problems with the law should disqualify him for athletic honors, Johnny Rodgers, Nebraska's three-time all-America, was named winner of the 1972 Heisman Memorial Trophy yesterday.

The all-purpose back was the greatest offensive player in college football history with 5,586 yards gained and 45 touchdowns in three years. However, some circles, especially in the East, had sought to deny him the Heisman because of his "bad boy" image.

In becoming the 38th recipient of the award, given to the outstanding college football player of the year by The Downtown Athletic Club here, Rodgers collected 301 first-place votes from the 934 electors (football writers and broadcasters) and a total of 1,310 points on the basis of 3 for a first place vote, 2 for a second and 1 for a third.

In second place was Greg Pruitt, Oklahoma's running back and the pre-season favorite for the award. Third was Rich Glover, a middle guard and Rodgers' teammate at Nebraska, making it a sweep for the Big Eight Conference.

The three are good friends, and Rodgers happened to be in Glover's home in Jersey City, N.J., when he heard the news.

"I suppose I'm surprised," he said. "I was hoping and wishing and imagining how it would be if I won it. It means a great deal in terms of pride, and also for me it seemed like for a while I wasn't going to get anything. At times I thought I wasn't even going to play anymore."

Rodgers' first brush with the law came at the end of his freshman year, when he and some friends held up a gasoline station, getting away with $90. Rodgers said it had been a "prank," but he was convicted, put on probation and had his driver's license revoked.

Later he was picked up and held on suspicion of possessing marijuana, although no evidence was found. Last spring he was arrested for running a stop light while driving with a suspended license. That case is still pending.

"I knew there was going to be a lot of controversy about all the trouble I had gotten into, but it was just something I felt I had to deal with," said Rodgers. "I understand how that goes. But I feel it was something that happened in the past. I feel that I have overcome this.

"I think it has made me a better man — although an older person at 21. It didn't matter to me if everybody thought Greg or Rich was a better football player on the field, but I would've hated to think that I didn't win the Heisman because of what had happened to me.

"Coach (Bob) Devaney has given me a lot of strength and confidence," said Rodgers, who grew up in the black section of Omaha, Neb. "He came out and said some things to defend me that he doesn't always say."

Rodgers has pro ambitions, but has no preference for any particular team.

THE 1973
ORANGE BOWL

62

Nebraska Hopes To Make Irish 3d Straight Orange Bowl Victim

By THE ASSOCIATED PRESS
The New York Times

MIAMI, December 31, 1972 — The prestige of the Big Eight Conference will be on the line when Nebraska seeks its third consecutive Orange Bowl victory tonight against Notre Dame.

The game will be nationally televised by the National Broadcasting Company beginning at 7:45 E.S.T.

The favored Cornhuskers, first in the college football polls the last two seasons, are down the list this year with a won-lost-tied record of 8-2-1.

But they could do a lot for the tarnished Big Eight reputation with a convincing victory over the Irish in what is expected to be a wide-open offensive battle. Three conference teams have lost in earlier bowl games.

"They're No. 4 in the nation in total defense and No. 4 in rushing defense," said the Notre Dame coach, Ara Parseghian, in referring to Nebraska.

"Also, as far as their offense and our defense is concerned, we didn't do a good job against Anthony Davis, and Nebraska has the Heisman Trophy winner in Johnny Rodgers, and Rodgers is a senior where Davis was only a sophomore," he said.

Davis scored six touchdowns when Southern California ripped Notre Dame, 45-23, in the final game of the season. But Parseghian isn't about to throw in the towel. He hasn't lost two games in a row since taking over at Notre Dame in 1964 and he has never suffered three losses in one season.

His offense has averaged 28 points a game, with Eric Penick, a sophomore, rushing for 727 yards, an average of 5.9 yards a carry. The fullback, Andy Huff, has been good for 4.9 yards a carry and 567 yards.

The sophomore quarterback, Tom Clements, has completed 51 percent of his passes for 1,163 yards and eight touchdowns.

Nebraska has been even more explosive, averaging 46 points a game with Rodgers accounting for 17 touchdowns, eight on pass receptions, seven rushing and two on punt returns.

The Cornhuskers, led by an all-America middle guard Rich Glover and Willie Harper, an all-America defensive end, have limited opponents to 91 points while posting four shutouts.

Notre Dame has recorded three shutouts and has allowed 152 points. But the offenses, rather than the defenses, should control the game.

The contest renews the series between the two schools which was interrupted in 1948 with the Irish leading seven victories to five. There was one tie.

Parseghian hopes to have better luck than Knute Rockne did. Rockne's famous Four Horsemen teams lost to Nebraska in 1922 and 1923, ruining unbeaten seasons for the Irish. They finally succeeded in the Four Horsemen's senior year, with a 34-6 rout of Nebraska.

63

Cornhuskers Romp Over Notre Dame In Orange Bowl

By BOB ELLIOTT
Special to The Miami Herald

MIAMI, January 1, 1973 — There have been some great contests and a few sleep-producing affairs in the history of the Orange Bowl Classic.

However, it's doubtful that any brought on deeper slumber than did Monday night's 39th offering which saw Nebraska's Cornhuskers smash Notre Dame's Fighting Irish in a 40-6 slaughter.

It was strictly no contest right from the start and was saved from complete oblivion only by a record-shattering performance by Nebraska's Heisman Memorial Trophy winner, Johnny Rodgers.

Rodgers scored four touchdowns and his 24 points set an Orange Bowl Classic record for scoring by an individual. The previous high of 19 points was set by Bobby Luna in Alabama's 61-6 rout of Syracuse back in 1953.

Rodgers, who sat out part of the third quarter and all of the fourth, ran for three touchdowns, caught a pass for another and along the way threw his only pass of the season for still another Nebraska six-pointer.

The capacity crowd of 80,010 and a national television audience saw Rodgers rush 15 times for 81 yards and catch three passes for 71 yards.

It was obvious that the Cornhuskers were determined to give Bob Devaney a victory in his final collegiate coaching job. However, it's doubtful that even the jovial Nebraska coach anticipated a rout of the proportions that developed.

The Cornhuskers scoring their third successive Orange Bowl victory, got seven points in the first quarter, 13 in the second period, and 20 in the third stanza.

Notre Dame finally succeeded in putting six points on the board early in the fourth quarter to avert the first Irish shutout since Nov. 27, 1965. The Irish had gone through 71 consecutive games without being blanked.

Strangely enough, the last time Notre Dame came away without scoring a point occurred right in this same Orange Bowl Stadium when the University of Miami fought the Irish to a scoreless tie.

The Cornhuskers shattered one Orange Bowl record of long standing. Their 30 first downs topped by one the total Alabama amassed in topping, of all teams, Nebraska, in 1966. Nebraska came close to a total offense mark, but its 560-yard total fell 28 yards short of the record 588 Alabama gained in crushing Syracuse. The Huskers got 300 yards rushing and 260 passing.

Notre Dame seemed simply to collapse after it failed to capitalize in the opening period.

After Nebraska had taken the opening kickoff back to its 24, the Huskers used 11 plays to march 76 yards to the first touchdown. Nebraska stayed on the ground for 10 of the plays, with Rodgers and Dave Goeller doing practically all of the ball-carrying.

Rodgers got the TD on an eight-yard burst over tackle, Rich Sanger converted and it was 7-0.

It looked as if the Irish might come right back with the equalizer as Tom Clements passed twice to Darryll Dewan for 12 and 29 yards. The last catch put the Irish on Nebraska's 20, but that was it.

On third down, Steve Manstedt tossed Clements for an eight-yard loss and Bob Thomas' 52-yard field goal try fell far short.

Near the end of the period, the Irish got their second chance. Goeller fumbled when hit by Kevin Nosbusch on a jarring tackle and Tim Sullivan covered for the Irish on Nebraska's 24.

Here again, on third down, Clements was tossed for a 13-yard loss by blitzing Dave Mason and the Irish had to punt.

It didn't appear to be the case at the time, but that was the absolute finish for Notre Dame.

Eleven plays later, Nebraska had gone 80 yards to its second touchdown.

With a 36-yard burst by Gary Dixon the piece de resistance, the Huskers moved to the Irish 20 and Humm flipped a pass to Bob

Revelle, who was downed on the one as the period ended.

Dixon leaped over guard on the second play of the second period for touchdown No. 2.

After the kickoff, Nebraska backed Notre Dame to its five-yard line and got the ball on a punt at the Husker 48.

From here, Humm flipped a lateral to Rodgers who passed downfield to Frosty Anderson, all alone at the Notre Dame 15. He just strolled into the end zone to make it 20-0.

The first time Nebraska got the ball into he second half, it scored again on a 42-yard drive. Rodgers was the big gun in this advance and he got the touchdown on a four-yard burst through the middle.

Nebraska went 80 yards for touchdown No. 5. Humm's passes ate up 41 of the yards, with Rodgers scoring from five yards out.

Rodgers, however, saved the best for his last.

With the ball on the 50, he took a lateral-type toss from Humm along the north sideline, outran one Notre Dame tackler after another and crossed the goal line untouched Irish defenders were sprawled all over the Orange Bowl turf as Rodgers crossed the goal line for the 50th touchdown of his collegiate career.

It was a fitting finish to a brilliant career.

It was after the final Nebraska score that Notre Dame finally got untracked.

The Irish ran the kickoff back to their 23 and finally got to the Nebraska 12 as the third period ended

Two running plays moved the ball to the five and, on third down, Clements passed to Pete Demmerle for the lone Irish touchdown.

A try for a two-point conversion failed, but this has to go down in Orange Bowl history as the lead of the "It Means Nothing" list.

SCORE BY PERIODS

Nebraska 7	13	20	0	—	40
Notre Dame.............0	0	0	6	—	6

64

Rodgers & Co. Smash Notre Dame

By GORDON S. WHITE Jr.
Special to The New York Times

MIAMI, January 1, 1973 — Johnny Rodgers showed why he was the Heisman Memorial Trophy winner as he led Nebraska to a shocking 40-6 victory over Notre Dame in the Orange Bowl tonight.

His four touchdowns and 24 points scored were records for one player in the Orange Bowl. He also tossed a touchdown pass on a spectacular 52-yard play before 80,010 persons and a national television audience.

Rodgers, who played tailback in the I formation for the first time in his college career, was the leader in a stunning team performance that swamped the Irish and established records against the team that has the tradition of picking on the other fellow most of the time.

It was a sweet finale for Bob Devaney. The Nebraska coach who now retires after 11 years of success at the helm of the Cornhuskers. But even if Nebraska had run up 1,000 points and set every record possible tonight, Devaney could not have the thing he wanted most when this season started — a record third straight national championship.

The victory was Nebraska's third straight Orange Bowl triumph in three years. But the 1971 and 1972 Orange triumphs made Nebraska No. 1 in the country each time. Tonight's game was just a big triumph over a usually strong team.

It was a dismal conclusion to the season for Notre Dame, which only last Dec. 2 suffered humiliation when Anthony Davis of Southern California set a record by scoring six touchdowns in the Trojans' 45-23 victory over Notre Dame.

Notre Dame yielded more records tonight as Nebraska's total offense of 560 yards (300 rushing, 260 passing) beat the previous high of 521 against an Irish team made by Michigan State in 1956. Nebraska's 30 first downs was an Orange Bowl record and a record against a Notre Dame team.

Ara Parseghian, Notre Dame's coach, said after the struggle, "When I see the films I will be able to evaluate the kind of game we played." Everyone else in the Orange Bowl tonight might be able to give him an idea of the kind of game the Irish played. They were never in it for a second.

Nebraska took the opening kickoff and drove 76 yards in 11 plays for the first score — a touchdown by Rodgers. Then the Cornhuskers defense held and back came Nebraska, driving Notre Dame into the Poly Turf. So it went, with Rodgers scoring three touchdowns in a span of 6 minutes 43 seconds in the third period.

Rodgers was superb as the leading rusher with 84 yards on 15 carries and leading receiver with 71 yards on three catches. Nebraska's second touchdown was scored by Gary Dixon on a 1-yard plunge at the end of an 80-yard drive. That was the only time Rodgers was not involved in the scoring.

The two fanciest of his touchdowns were on pass plays. Two and a half minutes after Dixon scored in the second quarter, Rodgers took a lateral from Dave Humm, the left-handed sophomore quarterback. Then Rodgers dropped back and let fly a long aerial to Frosty Anderson, who caught the ball at the 15 and ran over to complete that surprising 52-yard play.

Fine Individual Effort

Rodgers' final touchdown came when he took a short pass from Humm near the sideline and worked his way around frustrated Irish tacklers to score on a 50-yard play that was mostly running effort.

Notre Dame didn't score until early in the fourth period when Tom Clements passed 5 yards into the end zone to Pete Demmerle.

REMEMBERING
1971

65

'71 Huskers . . .
Best of the Best

By MIKE McKENZIE
The Sporting News

ST. LOUIS, Fall 1988 — Unlike most contests touted as the Game of the Century, the 1971 Nebraska-Oklahoma game truly lived up to its advance billing. What followed five weeks later was Game of the Century II, and though it failed, as do most sequels, to provide as much excitement as the Original, the spectacular result was a national champion that has come to be known as the greatest college football team of all time.

The Nebraska Cornhuskers emerged victorious from both holiday matchups — a Thanksgiving Day skim past Oklahoma, 35-31, and a New Year's Day crushing of Alabama, 38-6, in the Orange Bowl. The first triumph marked the only close call during a season in which the Huskers' slimmest margin of victory in their other games was 24 points, while the second sealed a second consecutive national championship.

"Most of the time, they just toyed with us," said Alabama Coach Paul (Bear) Bryant, whose previously undefeated and No. 2-ranked Crimson Tide was like putty in the hands of the Huskers. "They were one of the greatest (teams), if not the greatest, I have ever seen."

Coming from Bryant, who had played on Alabama's marvelous 1934 team and then coached three Crimson Tide squads to national championships in the 1960's, those words were powerful. They were echoed by Nebraska's coach, Bob Devaney.

"This is one of the greatest teams ever to play football," he said.

Seventeen years later, Devaney was pleased — but not surprised — to hear that his 1971 club had been selected as not just one of the greatest, but the greatest, in college gridiron history.

"We dominated every other team except Oklahoma with running, passing and defense," said Devaney, who retired as coach after the

1972 season but still serves as the Huskers' athletic director. "They really didn't have a bad game."

The Huskers hardly broke a sweat while executing almost flawlessly through 12 regular-season games and the Orange Bowl. In fact, the hard-fought battle between the Huskers and the Sooners produced only one penalty flag, a Nebraska offside. "It was a pretty intelligent group that didn't make many mistakes," Devaney said.

The Huskers also arrived at the stadium each week in a positive frame of mind, making Devaney's job that much easier. "One thing I remember so well is that we didn't have to juice 'em up," he said. "They didn't need any hype before games. Oh, if they had a bad half we'd get on their tails a little. But they played up to their capacity often, and most teams can't say that, even the good ones.

"Did we have a weakness? Not really."

Certainly not when it came to athletic ability. "The team wasn't especially big," he said, "but had an unusual amount of talent distributed both ways and a fine combination of passing and running. And then you add to that probably one of the best players who ever played anywhere. . . . It was an exceptional blend of personalities from all stations of life, too."

Indeed, Devaney's memories of his team center more on personalities than statistics, scores and strategies. Ironically, Nebraska's most vivid and controversial personality happened to be "one of the best players who ever played anywhere" — Johnny Rodgers.

Rodgers grew up on the north side of Omaha, where violence was a way of life. By the time he was 15 he already had been stabbed and had shot another boy in the stomach. If not for his excellence at sports, he looked like a good bet to wind up in prison — or the morgue.

But a football scholarship to Nebraska offered Rodgers a ticket out of the ghetto. He scored 11 touchdowns as a starting wingback in 1970 and appeared to be on his way to stardom.

After that sophomore season, however, Rodgers ran afoul of the law. It was discovered that a year earlier, he and some friends had robbed a gas station, netting the grand total of $91. "I didn't need the money," Rodgers later explained. "I had money in my pocket. It was just a challenge to see if we could do it."

Rodgers was sentenced to two years' probation. "He proved to be a good citizen in school on probation," Devaney said. "Credit (assistant coach) Tom Osborne with that, mostly. John hated two things —

running and getting up early in the morning. Tom would make John meet him at 6 A.M. and go for a little run if John was late to a meeting or something. That discouraged him, killed him."

Rodgers had additional brushes with the law while at Nebraska, but Devaney stood by him, taking considerable heat from the press in the process.

"John had a knack for being in the wrong place at the wrong time," the coach said, "except when he had a football in his hands."

At those times, Rodgers could take your breath away. As a runner, he juked his way around and sped right past entire defensive units. As a receiver, he had sure hands and an uncanny ability to get open. And as a kick returner, he was sensational. No matter how tightly he appeared to be hemmed in by would-be tacklers, he always seemed to find a way to wriggle free for a few more yards, if not a touchdown. "Probably the best wingback the college game has ever seen," Devaney said.

Rodgers was not averse to the spotlight, which was fortunate for the Huskers. He was driven to reach the end zone.

"We had such a good team," he explained, "that . . . I was desperate. I didn't want to carry it to the 5 or 10 so that someone else could take it in. Every time I got the ball, I wanted to score."

As a junior in 1971, Rodgers led the Huskers in scoring with 17 touchdowns, including three on punt returns, one on a kickoff return and 11 on pass receptions. He earned consensus all-America honors for the first of two years.

"John wasn't big," Devaney said, "but tremendously strong and he carried people along with him. A great competitor, too. I half-kiddingly told him before his junior year he could win the Heisman, and he laughed."

Rodgers did win The Heisman Memorial Trophy as a senior, an accomplishment that would have seemed impossible during his troubled teen-age years. Perhaps most surprised by his rise to prominence was Rodgers himself.

"John always pictured himself as a dead-end kid," Devaney said. "We had some dead-end kids, for sure."

Rich Glover, for instance.

"It was bad in Jersey City," recalled Glover, a middle guard from New Jersey. "Not real bad, but bad, and got worse. I always dreamed of getting away from home and seeing some good things, and Nebraska made it possible."

That was just a stroke of luck. Husker coaches, who were forced to recruit nationally because of Nebraska's small population, saw him by chance while scouting offensive tackle Daryl White in East Orange, N.J. Apparently, no other major schools were aware of him, either, because Nebraska was the only one that offered Glover a scholarship.

Stardom did not come quickly to Glover. He was a second-string tackle his sophomore season, when the Huskers' Orange Bowl triumph over Louisiana State won them the top spot in the final Associated Press poll. (United Press International, which published its final rankings before New Year's Day upsets of Texas and Ohio State, had the 1970 Huskers rated third.) Entering the 1971 season, Glover was lost in a shuffle of defensive linemen. Then one day at practice, Devaney instructed his staff to move Glover to the middle, where the departure of All-Big Eight Conference pick Eddie Periard had created a vacancy. Glover played middle guard with such demonic fury, Devaney left him there.

"I believe he was the best at his position in the 70's," Devaney said. "Some opponents never even knew how tough he was because he was so quick, they never touched him."

Glover earned all-conference honors in 1971, a year before he won both the Outland Trophy and the Lombardi Award. The '71 Outland winner was another Nebraska player, consensus all-America defensive tackle Larry Jacobson.

Like Glover, Jacobson became a much better player than Devaney ever had anticipated. In fact, after Devaney left Jacobson's home in Sioux Falls, S.D., on a recruiting trip, he told his wife, "He looks like a sissy." Jacobson wore homed-rimmed glasses and had a baby face, but his development into a defensive terror taught Devaney a lesson.

"I learned with him not ever to pick a guy on what he looks like," he said. "Jake just had a soft, quiet personality, and on film he looked like he kind of sloughed off, but he was a gamer underneath."

An unassuming gamer. His reaction to the news that he had become Nebraska's first Outland Trophy winner was more confusion than exultation. "Nobody even knew for sure how to spell it," Jacobson said, "let alone what it was." Nebraska's other consensus all-America in '71 was defensive end Willie Harper, who "belongs in the same class with Jacobson and Glover," Devaney said. The Toledo, Ohio, native made 66 tackles that year, including a team-high 18 behind the line of scrimmage.

Harper, Jacobson and Glover were the big three on a defensive line that was second to none. They and tackle Bill Janssen and end John Adkins combined for 61 tackles for 301 yards in losses.

Nebraska's top linebacker was Bob Terrio, a junior college transfer who, like Glover, found his niche after a position change. He had been tried at fullback, his high school and junior college specialty, before switching to defense. Terrio, the team's leading tackler with 96, and Jim Branch formed a solid linebacking corps.

One of the strongest but least publicized segments of the Nebraska team was the defensive secondary. The Huskers intercepted 27 passes in '71, compared with only six by their opponents. Largely responsible for that advantage were safety Bill Kosch, cornerbacks Joe Blahak and Jim Anderson and monster back Dave Mason, whom Devaney touted to be "as good as Nebraska has ever had at monster."

Mason and Anderson both hailed from Green Bay, Wis., where Devaney got some important help in his recruiting efforts from a man named Henry Atkinson.

"He was a brother to the mayor of Green Bay when we got to know him, a big Packers fan," Devaney said. "He took to Nebraska for some reason and helped us with some recruits out of Green Bay."

Not just any recruits, but future starters: Anderson, the defensive captain, and Mason, plus quarterback Jerry Tagge, an Omaha native who later moved to Green Bay.

Tagge, the offensive captain, had only half of a starting job when the '71 season opened. He and Van Brownson had shared time for two years, and two seniors alternating at quarterback appealed to Devaney. Brownson was the better runner, but Tagge was almost as good, plus he held almost every school passing record after just two years of part-time duty. As the season progressed, Tagge assumed the leading role and rose to No. 1 draft status with his hometown team, the Packers.

Tagge ran the offense beautifully, picking most of the plays himself and often calling audibles at the line of scrimmage. "Devaney and Tom Osborne trained me, and I thought like Bob did," Tagge said. "We would do the same thing in the same situations. He turned it over to me." Tagge's knack for calling the right play at the right time was a big key to the Huskers' success. "The thing about Jerry," guard Dick Rupert told a reporter that year, "is that he listens to you.

He trusts you in the huddle to tell what might work. If I give him a nod, he knows I'm handling my guy and he can run there."

The Huskers lined up in various sets out of the I-formation, making it hard for defenses to get a good read on the play. Even more troublesome than multiple sets were the multiple talents of Tagge's chief ball handlers — the shifty Rodgers, I-backs Jeff Kinney and Gary Dixon, fullbacks Bill Olds and Maury Damkroger, split end Woody Cox and tight end Jerry List. The runners could catch and the receivers could run, lending balance to an already vigorous attack.

The big-play man was Rodgers, but Kinney could do just as much damage. He accumulated more rushing/receiving yards (1,289) than anybody on the team and scored 16 touchdowns while doing everything from line crashes to pass patterns. By season's end he had become the school's career rushing leader and No. 2 career receiver.

Though just a junior, Rodgers already was first in the latter department. He hauled in 53 passes for 872 yards in '71, but opponents who decided to key on Rodgers were in for trouble. Cox (24 catches), Kinney (23) and List (21) made good targets, too.

Less spectacular but even more productive than Nebraska's passing game was its rushing. Kinney led the way with 1,037 yards, while Olds and Dixon combined for 1,001 yards. Tagge and Rodgers chipped in with another 573.

These numbers were of more interest to opponents than they were to the Huskers, who went about their business with level heads and small egos. "We don't have any stars on the team," Tagge said midway through the season. "We just have a lot of good football players who concentrate and carry out their assignments." That may have been the intention, but Tagge, Rodgers, Kinney, Jacobson, Glover and Harper were emerging as stars of the country's strongest team anyway.

The unsung heroes of the Nebraska offense were the linemen. Called "my saviors many times" by Tagge, the line featured White and Carl Johnson at tackle, Rupert and Keith Wortman at guard and Doug Dumler at center. They were "really tight, close, the heart and soul of our team." Tagge said, "the hardest workers but always cutting up, and inseparable. . . . They knew where each other was every minute of the day, and that was mostly in the weight-lifting room."

Two of those linemen were among four recruits who had surprised Devaney by enrolling at Nebraska in the first place. When the prospects, who had played junior college ball in such warm climates as California, Arizona and New Mexico, first visited Lincoln, they had been welcomed by a fierce winter storm.

"It snowed and blowed, and I figured we wasted our money, we'd never see them again," Devaney said. "But all four came and were starters on that '71 team — Dick Rupert, Woody Cox, Carl Johnson and Bob Terrio."

That Devaney wound up as head coach at Nebraska was a bit of a surprise, too. After graduating from Alma (Mich.) College in 1939, he spent 14 years coaching high school football before getting his first taste of the college game as an assistant at Michigan State. Four years later, he was hired as head coach at Wyoming. His Cowboy teams posted a 35-10-5 record in five years, attracting the attention of officials at Nebraska, where fans had cheered only three winning seasons in the previous 21 years. Devaney was hired in 1962.

Devaney was such an unknown when he came to Lincoln that people used a slogan to remind themselves how to pronounce his name: "Get off your fanny and help Devaney." But Nebraskans caught on quickly as his first team went 9-2 and won the Gotham Bowl. When he retired as coach a decade later, none of his teams ever had experienced a losing season and the school had its first two national championships.

The first, in 1970, sent the state into a frenzy. Almost anything in red that featured a "1" displayed prominently was a guaranteed big seller. And with expectations high for a repeat performance in '71, Husker hysteria intensified. The hype even prompted Devaney to declare an official Back-to-Earth Day for his squad. "Over-confidence never became a problem, though," he reflected years later.

Even after squashing their first seven opponents to set up an important Big Eight encounter with once-defeated Colorado, the Huskers stayed cool and worked hard. The ninth-ranked Buffaloes were the first big test for the Huskers, who came through with flying colors in a physical 31-7 victory.

Easy wins the next two weeks boosted Nebraska's record to 10-0. The combined score of those no-contests stood 389-64, including three shutouts, and the Huskers rested comfortably atop the polls. Rated second was Oklahoma, which had overwhelmed all nine of its opponents prior to its November 25 date with Nebraska in Norman. The stage was set for a showdown at the O.U. Corral.

The media blitz preceding the latest Game of the Century focused on the strengths of the two combatants: Nebraska had the nation's No. 1 defense, but the question was whether it could stop an Oklahoma triple-option offense that was unsurpassed in rushing yards, total yards and scoring. With Jack Mildren at quarterback and the amazing Greg Pruitt, Joe Wylie (or Roy Bell) and Leon Crosswhite behind him, Sooners Coach Chuck Fairbanks had more speed in his backfield than any wishbone coach ever. The Huskers' well-balanced offense was not ignored, but many believed that Oklahoma could simply outscore Nebraska, great defense or not.

All of the prognosticating was somewhat lost on the Huskers, who saw the game as a big one, but nothing monumental.

"We never realized the significance of everything at the time," Tagge said. "Geez, we were all kids who just lived together and played together. There was no big pressure because we were having so much fun.

"It took a lot of work on our part to accomplish all we did, but we never thought of it as work. It was good times. At the time I remember simply thinking it was neat; then, all of a sudden, I find myself a better-than-average player on a great team. A lot of us felt that way.

"I sure never anticipated all the hoopla that would stay with that team. I answer more questions about the 1971 team now than I did in 1971. Especially one game."

That game was watched on national television by more than 55 million people — the largest TV audience ever to watch a college football game — as well as 63,385 fans at Oklahoma Memorial Stadium on a gorgeous autumn afternoon. But the weather didn't keep some of the participants from getting the jitters.

"I remember being very, very cold before the game," Tagge said. "Nothing was going through my mind. I was blanked out."

Until the opening kickoff. "It meant the buildup was over," he said. "Once the game started, we relaxed."

Said Jacobson: "My legs were like rubber at the start, we were so high, and we didn't wake up until the second quarter."

The team as a whole, perhaps, but not Rodgers. Just 31 minutes into the game, his punt return for a touchdown gave Nebraska the edge it needed in a game in which each side launched four TD drives and Oklahoma added a field goal.

Rodgers ran 72 yards for the score. Some of the yards he covered falling down, some spinning and the last chunk in an all-out sprint. Afterward, on the sideline, he threw up.

"Of all the thousands of plays I've seen in college football," Devaney said, "I probably have to rate that punt return the best. I've watched it so many times on film, I've got it memorized. It's gotten bigger and bigger over the years. . . .

"What I remember most was that Wylie kicked it high and I thought John should have made a fair catch. It never entered his mind."

He fielded the punt and immediately absorbed a hit by Pruitt, who unwittingly spun Rodgers away from the almost certain grasp of teammate Ken Jones. Rodgers nearly went down but steadied himself with one hand on the artificial turf. The return was set up to the right, but Rodgers cut to the left and ran through a horde of would be tacklers. He motored down the left sideline with only one man left to beat — the punter, Wylie — and Blahak bumped him out of the way.

"John could have crawled in after that," Devaney said.

Rich Sanger's kick made it 74. Oklahoma closed the gap to 7-3 on a 30-yard field goal, but the Huskers took a 14-3 lead on Kinney's one-yard plunge after the offense finally started clicking in the second quarter.

"Both teams got better as the game wore on," Tagge said. "I remember us being behind at halftime, and we hadn't been behind at all."

Indeed, Nebraska trailed for the first time all season when the Sooners took a 17-14 lead just before the end of the half. Mildren ran the ball in from two yards out for the first tally and then connected with Jon Harrison, his high school teammate from Abilene, Tex., on a 24-yard scoring toss.

Surprisingly, Nebraska was doing an excellent job controlling the Sooners' running game. The ends, Harper and Adkins, were denying Pruitt and the other backs any chance to sweep outside. But Devaney's preoccupation with stopping that aspect of the triple option left the Huskers vulnerable to the pass.

"They had an outstanding wide receiver (Harrison), and my staff — Warren Powers, Monte Kiffin and John Melton on defense — decided we needed to cover him with our best man," Devaney said. "So we switched Joe Blahak from corner to safety (to defend against the run) and went man for man (with Kosch on Harrison), where we had been in a zone all year.

"It didn't work. We didn't compensate with a good blitz. Every time they needed yards, they threw to that wide receiver. I'm not taking anything away from their offense, but we could handle Jack

Mildren and Greg Pruitt, and those passes made the score closer than it should have been. We helped Oklahoma with some erroneous planning, and we were all in on it."

Nebraska regained the lead, 28-17, on a pair of short runs by Kinney in the third quarter. An 11-point lead ordinarily would have been plenty, but the Husker defense continued to bend when pressed by Oklahoma's powerful wishbone. Mildren scored again on a three-yard run, and his 16-yard pass to Harrison gave the Sooners their second lead of the day, 31-28, with 7:10 left in the game.

Time was slipping away, but the Huskers didn't panic. They just took a deep breath and went to work, starting at their own 26-yard line.

"I thought we could score," Devaney said, "because our offense had been moving the ball in the second half."

In this key drive, Nebraska's mover and shaker was Kinney. Tagge kept giving him the ball, and Kinney responded valiantly, thanks to a lesson he had learned in an earlier game.

"I gave Jeff the ball four ar five times in a row," Tagge recalled of that previous incident. "He came back and said, 'Give it to somebody else, I'm tired.' I made him run it again. He went 35 yards for a touchdown. When he came to the sideline, I said: 'Now you can rest. If you're going to be in my huddle, you have to be ready.' Jeff never said that again. Against Oklahoma he was, 'Jerry, give me the ball,' and I had to calm him down."

After Rodgers ran four yards on a first-down reverse, Tagge gave the ball to Kinney, who shook off Sooner defenders for gains of five and 17 yards to move inside Oklahoma territory. Dixon then rushed for two yards, pushing Nebraska to the Oklahoma 46, but Tagge's pass to Rodgers on second down went out of bounds. The Huskers needed eight yards for a first down to keep the drive alive.

"When it came to third and eight," Tagge said, "He knew just where to slide into their defense. I was scrambling, the play was broken, but Johnny sensed it like always. He had that knack of finding the open spot."

Rodgers found it, slid to his knees as Tagge threw low and gathered in the ball with his fingertips for an 11-yard gain and first down at the Oklahoma 35.

Except for a Rodgers reverse that netted seven yards, Tagge went exclusively with Kinney the rest of the way. The I-back continued to blast through would-be tacklers when given the ball five more times, four of them to the same spot opened by White at left tackle. He accounted for 50 of the 74 yards in the 12-play drive, including the last two for the touchdown with 1:38 remaining. It was the fourth TD of the day for Kinney, who finished with 174 yards rushing on 3 1 carries.

Oklahoma trailed, 35-31, with one last chance to knock off the top-ranked team in the land. But when Glover deflected Mildren's pass on fourth and 14, the Huskers were free to run out the clock.

"Kinney and Rodgers and Tagge got all the attention, but we never would have stopped Oklahoma that day without Richie," Devaney said. "He smashed their inside game. He had 22 tackles. The TV cameras couldn't help but be on him all day long."

The Game of the Century was over. The Huskers were still No. 1, not to mention Big Eight champions, and the state of Nebraska went wild.

"When we flew back to Lincoln," Jacobson said, "the plane couldn't get us to the terminal because of the people on the runway. It was bedlam."

Nebraska completed its regular season with a trip to Honolulu and a 45-3 romp over Hawaii for its 31st consecutive game without a defeat. The Huskers' last test would come in the Orange Bowl against an 114 Alabama team that had risen to second in the polls after the Sooners' loss to Nebraska

The Game of the Century II matched Devaney, a relative newcomer to the national championship scene, against Paul (Bear) Bryant, who already listed three national crowns on his lengthy resume. Few people realized at the time that Devaney had a better coaching record than Bryant, perhaps because Bryant's Crimson Tide had whipped Nebraska in the 1966 Orange Bowl and 1967 Sugar Bowl.

"A lot of people thought we were psyched out and couldn't beat Bear," Devaney said, "so it was especially satisfying when we found out we could."

Devaney allowed his players to cut loose while visiting Miami. Reports had them horsing around in the pool, betting at the horse and dog tracks and taking in other sights around town.

"We want them to have fun and not impress on them the personal importance I feel about this game," Devaney said at the time. "I've lost twice to Bear, and I don't like to think there's a guy who can just walk out on the field and beat me any time he wants to, even if his team is very good. Fortunately, our players aren't as aware of the stigma as we coaches, because they were only in high school when

Bear beat us in the '60s." Bryant, who kept a tight rein on his players in Miami, had switched to the wishbone in the intervening years. But even with Johnny Musso in the backfield, Alabama's wishbone paled in comparison to Oklahoma's, making Nebraska a strong favorite for the national title.

"We didn't feel like Alabama could push us like Oklahoma did," Devaney said. "We felt Alabama lacked team speed. . . . I was scared going down there, because of the past, and not at all overconfident. But the plain, cold facts were, we were better."

And it showed. Nebraska had no trouble shutting down the wishbone while running roughshod over a Crimson Tide defense that ranked higher than any the Huskers had faced all season. Rodgers repeated his favorite trick by returning a punt 77 yards for a touchdown on the last play of the first quarter, and Nebraska led, 14-0, on its way to a 28-0 halftime romp. The last 30 minutes were just a formality. "As a matter of fact," Rodgers said, "a few of us talked at the half about a celebration party we were going to have back at the hotel."

Before the celebration however, came a touching moment in the Nebraska locker room. Moments after the Huskers sealed their second straight national championship with the 38-6 victory, Rodgers jumped up on a bench in the middle of a cluster of reporters, held a ball over his head and shouted, "The game ball should go to one of the greatest guys there is, Rex Lowe."

Lowe was a Husker split end who had contracted Hodgkin's disease. When Rodgers saw Lowe roll into the dressing room in a wheelchair, he gave the ball to his teammate. The two embraced in silence, tears rolling down their cheeks.

Over in the other dressing room, a living legend of a coach, after absorbing his worst beating at Alabama and almost of his career, was saying to all who could decipher his mumbles: "We were just beaten by a great football team. . . . They just flat whipped our butts in every way known to man."

Great teams have a penchant for doing that — and the Huskers were the best ever.

THE
APPENDIX

Honors

NATIONAL CHAMPIONS 1970, 1971

BIG EIGHT CHAMPIONS 1963, 1964, 1965, 1966,
1969, 1970, 1971, 1972

HEISMAN TROPHY WINNER . . . . Johnny Rodgers, 1972

OUTLAND TROPHY WINNERS . . . . Larry Jacobson, 1971
Rich Glover, 1972

LOMBARDI AWARD WINNER . . . . Rich Glover, 1972

ALL-AMERICA

YEAR	PLAYER	POSITION
1963	Bob Brown	Guard
1964	Larry Kramer	Tackle
1965	Walt Barnes	Tackle
1965	Tony Jeter	End
1965	Freeman White	End
1966	LaVerne Allers	Guard
1966	Larry Wachholtz	Defensive Back
1966	Wayne Meylan	Middle Guard
1967	Wayne Meylan	Middle Guard
1968	Joe Armstrong	Guard
1970	Jerry Murtaugh	Linebacker
1970	Bob Newton	Tackle
1971	Jeff Kinney	I-Back
1971	Larry Jacobson	Tackle
1971	Jerry Tagge	Quarterback
1971	Rich Glover	Middle Guard
1971	Willie Harper	Defensive End
1971	Johnny Rodgers	Wingback
1972	Rich Glover	Middle Guard
1972	Willie Harper	Defensive End
1972	Johnny Rodgers	Wingback
1972	Daryl White	Tackle

N.F.L. Draftees

YEAR	PLAYER	ROUND	TEAM
1963	Dennis Claridge	3	Green Bay
1963	Bill Thornton	11	St. Louis
1963	Dave Theisen	11	Los Angeles
1964	Bob Brown	1	Philadelphia
1964	Lloyd Voss	1	Green Bay
1964	Rudy Johnson	5	San Francisco
1964	John Kirby	5	Minnesota
1964	Willie Ross	9	St. Louis
1964	Monte Kiffin	15	Minnesota
1964	Larry Kramer	15	Baltimore
1964	Robert Jones	18	Washington
1964	Bob Hohn	20	Los Angeles
1965	Kent McCloughan	3	Washington
1965	John Strohmeyer	12	Washington
1965	Preston Love	19	Detroit
1966	Walt Barnes	2	Washington
1966	Tony Jeter	3	Green Bay
1966	Bob Pickens	3	Chicago
1966	Dick Czap	12	Cleveland
1966	James Brown	13	St. Louis
1966	Lynn Senkbeil	16	Chicago
1966	Dick Fitzgerald	19	San Francisco
1967	Harry Wilson	3	Philadelphia
1967	Carl Stith	4	Houston
1967	Ron Kirkland	9	Baltimore
1967	Pete Tatman	10	Minnesota
1967	Kaye Carstens	13	Chicago
1968	Wayne Meylan	4	Cleveland

YEAR	PLAYER	ROUND	TEAM
1968	Ben Gregory	5	Buffalo
1968	Bob Taucher	7	Dallas
1969	James Hawkins	7	Los Angeles
1969	Dick Davis	12	Cleveland
1970	Jim McFarland	7	St. Louis
1970	Ken Geddes	7	Detroit
1970	Dana Stephenson	8	Chicago
1970	Mike Wynn	8	Oakland
1970	Frank Patrick	10	Green Bay
1970	Bob Liggett	15	Kansas City
1970	Mike Green	16	San Diego
1970	Glenn Patterson	17	Dallas
1971	Joe Orduna	2	San Francisco
1971	Bob Newton	3	Chicago
1971	Paul Rogers	8	Pittsburgh
1971	Dan Schneiss	12	New England
1972	Jerry Tagge	1	Green Bay
1972	Jeff Kinney	1	Kansas City
1972	Larry Jacobson	1	Giants
1972	Carl Johnson	5	New Orleans
1972	Van Brownson	8	Baltimore
1972	Keith Wortman	10	Green Bay
1973	Johnny Rodgers	1	San Diego
1973	Willie Harper	2	San Francisco
1973	Monte Johnson	2	Oakland
1973	Bill Olds	3	Baltimore
1973	Rich Glover	3	Giants
1973	Doug Dumler	5	New England
1973	Joe Blahak	8	Houston
1973	Bill Janssen	8	Pittsburgh
1973	Dave Mason	10	Minnesota
1973	Jerry List	11	Oakland

The Bob Devaney Record
At The University of Nebraska

1962

(9-2-0)

Captains: Bob Thornton, Dwain Carlson

Sept. 22	W	South Dakota	53-0	H
Sept. 29	W	Michigan	25-13	A
Oct. 6	W	Iowa State	36-22	H
Oct. 13	W	North Carolina State	19-14	H
Oct. 20	W	Kansas State	26-6	H
Oct. 27	W	Colorado	31-6	A
Nov. 3	L	Missouri	7-16	H
Nov. 10	W	Kansas	40-16	A
Nov. 17	W	Oklahoma State	14-0	H
Nov. 24	L	Oklahoma	6-34	A

GOTHAM BOWL

Dec. 15	W	Miami (Fla.)	36-34	N

N — at Yankee Stadium, New York City.

1963

(10-1-0)

BIG EIGHT CHAMPIONS

Captains: Dennis Claridge, John Kirby

Sept. 21	W	South Dakota State	58-7	H
Sept. 28	W	Minnesota	14-7	A
Oct. 5	W	Iowa State	21-7	H
Oct. 12	L	Air Force	13-17	H
Oct. 19	W	Kansas State	28-6	A
Oct. 26	W	Colorado	41-6	H
Nov. 2	W	Missouri	13-12	A
Nov. 9	W	Kansas	23-9	H
Nov. 16	W	Oklahoma State	20-16	A
Nov. 23	W	Oklahoma	29-20	H

ORANGE BOWL

Jan. 1	W	Auburn	13-7	N

N — at Miami, Fla.

1964
(9-2-0)
BIG EIGHT CHAMPIONS
Captains: Lyle Sittler, Bobby Hohn

Sept. 19	W	South Dakota	56-0	H
Sept. 26	W	Minnesota	26-21	A
Oct. 3	W	Iowa State	14-7	A
Oct. 10	W	South Carolina	28-6	H
Oct. 17	W	Kansas State	47-0	H
Oct. 24	W	Colorado	21-3	A
Oct. 31	W	Missouri	9-0	H
Nov. 7	W	Kansas	14-7	A
Nov. 14	W	Oklahoma State	27-14	H
Nov. 21	L	Oklahoma	7-17	A

COTTON BOWL

Jan. 1	L	Arkansas	7-10	N

N — at Dallas, Tex.

1965
(10-1-0)
BIG EIGHT CHAMPIONS
Captains: Frank Solich, Mike Kennedy

Sept. 18	W	Texas Christian	34-14	H
Sept. 25	W	Air Force	27-17	A
Oct. 2	W	Iowa State	44-0	H
Oct. 9	W	Wisconsin	37-0	H
Oct. 16	W	Kansas State	41-0	A
Oct. 23	W	Colorado	38-13	H
Oct. 30	W	Missouri	16-14	A
Nov. 6	W	Kansas	42-6	H
Nov. 13	W	Oklahoma State	21-17	A
Nov. 20	W	Oklahoma	21-9	H

ORANGE BOWL

Jan. 1	L	Alabama	28-39	N

N — at Miami, Fla.

1966

(9-2-0)

BIG EIGHT CHAMPIONS

Captains: Bob Churchich, Larry Wachholtz

Sept. 17	W	Texas Christian	14-10	H
Sept. 24	W	Utah State	28-7	H
Oct. 1	W	Iowa State	12-6	A
Oct. 8	W	Wisconsin	31-3	A
Oct. 15	W	Kansas State	21-10	H
Oct. 22	W	Colorado	21-19	A
Oct. 29	W	Missouri	35-0	H
Nov. 5	W	Kansas	24-13	A
Nov. 12	W	Oklahoma State	21-6	H
Nov. 19	L	Oklahoma	9-10	A

SUGAR BOWL

Jan. 2	L	Alabama	7-34	N

N — at New Orleans, La.

1967

(6-4-0)

Captains: Ben Gregory, Marv Mueller

Sept. 16	W	Washington	17-0	A
Sept. 30	W	Minnesota	7-0	H
Oct. 7	W	Kansas State	16-14	A
Oct. 14	L	Kansas	0-10	A
Oct. 21	L	Colorado	16-21	H
Oct. 28	W	Texas Christian	29-0	A
Nov. 4	W	Iowa State	12-0	H
Nov. 11	W	Oklahoma State	9-0	H
Nov. 18	L	Missouri	7-10	A
Nov. 25	L	Oklahoma	14-21	H

1968
(6-4-0)

Captains: Tom Penney, Jim Hawkins

Sept. 14	W	Wyoming	13-10	H
Sept. 21	W	Utah	31-0	H
Oct. 28	W	Minnesota	17-14	A
Oct. 12	L	Kansas	13-23	H
Oct. 19	L	Missouri	14-16	H
Oct. 26	W	Oklahoma State	21-20	A
Nov. 2	W	Iowa State	24-13	A
Nov. 9	L	Kansas State	0-12	H
Nov. 16	W	Colorado	22-6	A
Nov. 23	L	Oklahoma	0-47	A

1969
(9-2-0)

BIG EIGHT CHAMPIONS

Captains: Mike Green, Dana Stephenson

Sept. 20	L	Southern California	21-31	H
Sept. 27	W	Texas A&M	14-0	H
Oct. 4	W	Minnesota	42-14	A
Oct. 11	L	Missouri	7-17	A
Oct. 18	W	Kansas	21-17	H
Oct. 25	W	Oklahoma State	13-3	H
Nov. 1	W	Colorado	20-7	H
Nov. 8	W	Iowa State	17-3	H
Nov. 15	W	Kansas State	10-7	A
Nov. 22	W	Oklahoma	44-14	A

SUN BOWL

| Dec. 20 | W | Georgia | 45-6 | N |

N — at El Paso, Tex.

1970
(11-0-1)
NATIONAL CHAMPIONS
BIG EIGHT CHAMPIONS
Captains: Dan Schneiss, Jerry Murtaugh

Sept. 12	W	Wake Forest	36-12	H
Sept. 19	T	Southern California	21-21	A
Sep. 26	W	Army	28-0	H
Oct. 3	W	Minnesota	35-10	A
Oct. 10	W	Missouri	21-7	H
Oct. 17	W	Kansas	41-20	A
Oct. 24	W	Oklahoma State	65-31	H
Oct. 31	W	Colorado	29-13	A
Nov. 7	W	Iowa State	54-29	A
Nov. 16	W	Kansas State	51-13	H
Nov. 21	W	Oklahoma	28-21	H

ORANGE BOWL
Jan. 1	W	Louisiana State	17-12	N

N — at Miami, Fla.

1971
(13-0-0)
NATIONAL CHAMPIONS
BIG EIGHT CHAMPIONS
Captains: Jerry Tagge, Jim Anderson

Sept. 11	W	Oregon	34-7	H
Sept. 18	W	Minnesota	35-7	H
Sep. 25	W	Texas A&M	34-7	H
Oct. 2	W	Utah State	42-6	H
Oct. 9	W	Missouri	36-0	A
Oct. 16	W	Kansas	55-0	H
Oct. 23	W	Oklahoma State	41-13	A
Oct. 30	W	Colorado	31-7	H
Nov. 6	W	Iowa State	37-0	H
Nov. 13	W	Kansas State	44-17	A
Nov. 25	W	Oklahoma	35-31	A
Dec. 4	W	Hawaii	45-3	A

ORANGE BOWL
Jan. 1	W	Alabama	38-6	N

N — at Miami, Fla.

1972
(9-2-1)
BIG EIGHT CHAMPIONS
Captains: Doug Dumler, Bill Janssen

Date				Site
Sept. 9	L	U.C.L.A.	17-20	A
Sept. 16	W	Texas A&M	37-7	H
Sep. 23	W	Army	77-7	A
Sep. 30	W	Minnesota	49-0	H
Oct. 14	W	Missouri	62-0	H
Oct. 21	W	Kansas	56-0	A
Oct. 28	W	Oklahoma State	34-0	H
Nov. 4	W	Colorado	33-10	A
Nov. 11	T	Iowa State	23-23	A
Nov. 18	W	Kansas State	59-7	H
Nov. 23	L	Oklahoma	14-17	H

ORANGE BOWL

Jan. 1	W	Notre Dame	40-6	N

N — at Miami, Fla.

VARSITY MONOGRAMS

Listed below are the names of the University of Nebraska varsity monogram winners during the Bob Devaney era of 1962 to 1972. For example, in the listing of Robert Churchich, the years are 1964-66, meaning Churchich lettered in 1964, 1965 and 1966.

A

John Adkins	1970-71
LaVerne Allers	1964-66
Barry Alvarez	1965-67
Tom Alward	1972-74
Dan Anderson	1972
Frosty Anderson	1971-72
Jim Anderson	1969-71
Joe Armstrong	1966-68
Carl Ashman	1967-69
Al Austin	1971-72
Frank Avolio	1967-68

B

James Baffico	1962
Ritch Bahe	1972
Walter Barnes	1963-65
John Bell	1972
Mike Beran	1970-72
Bob Best	1966-68
Joe Blahak	1970-72
Bill Bomberger	1967
Randy Borg	1971-72
Jim Branch	1970-72
Gary Brichacek	1964-66
Mel Brichacek	1966-68
James Brown	1964-65
Robert Brown	1962-63
Van Brownson	1969-71
Kenny Brunk	1965-66
George Buckler	1967
Joe Buda	1968-69

C

Richard Callahan	1962-63
Dennis Carlson	1964-65
Dwain Carlson	1962
Jim Carstens	1970-71
Kaye Carstens	1964-66
Larry Casey	1965
Robert Churchich	1964-66
Dennis Claridge	1962-63
Langston Coleman	1964-66
Richard Coleman	1965-66
William Comstock	1962
Woody Cox	1970-71
Marvin Crenshaw	1972
Richard Czap	1964-66

D

Maury Damkroger	1971-72
Dick Davis	1966-68
John Decker	1968-70
Dan Delaney	1966, 68
John Dervin	1962-64
Dale Didur	1971
Gary Dixon	1971-72
Mark Doak	1972
Charles Doepke	1963-64
Larry Donovan	1962
Ron Drakulich	1968-69
Duncan Drum	1963-65
Fred Duda	1963-65
Rich Duda	1972
Doug Dumler	1970-72
John Dutton	1971-72
Tony Dvorsak	1969

E		**I**	
Mike Eger	1962	Guy Ingles	1968-70
F		**J**	
John Faiman	1962	Larry Jacobson	1969-71
Adrian Fiala	1967-69	Doug Jamail	1970-71
Pat Fischer	1972	Leonard Janik	1965-67
Richard Fischer	1962	Bill Janssen	1969, 71-72
Larry Frost	1967-69	Sherwin Jarmon	1968-69
		Tony Jeter	1963-65
G		Ardell Johnson	1972
Dennis Galbraith	1969	Carl Johnson	1970-71
Glen Garson	1971-72	Doug Johnson	1970
Jim Gatziolis	1967	Monte Johnson	1970-72
Ken Geddes	1967-69	Rudy Johnson	1962-63
Rich Glover	1970-72	William Johnson	1963-65
Dave Goeller	1972	Robert Jones	1963
Mike Grace	1964-65		
Mike Green	1968-69	**K**	
Ben Gregory	1965-67	Michael Kennedy	1963-65
Bob Grenfell	1969-70	Monte Kiffin	1962-63
Ronald Griesse	1963-64	Miles Kimmel	1966, 68
Dermis Gutzman	1968	Jeff Kinney	1969-71
		John Kinsel	1972
H		John Kirby	1962-63
Ed Hansen	1967-68	Ron Kirkland	1964-66
Willie Harper	1970-72	Dan Kobza	1967-68
Phil Harvey	1970-71	John Koinzan	1963-64
William Haug	1963-65	Bill Kosch	1969-71
Bruce Hauge	1970-71	Larry Kramer	1962-64
James Hawkins	1967-68	Roger Kudrna	1965, 67
Stan Hegener	1972	Alan Kuehl	1965-67
Tom Heller	1968	George Kyros	1972
Jeff Hill	1972		
Robert Hill	1965-66	**L**	
Robert Hohn	1963-64	Al Larson	1967-69
Gary Hollstein	1970-71	Bob Liggett	1968-69
Bill Hornbacher	1968-69	Tom Linstroth	1968
James Huge	1962	Bob Lints	1966
Jeff Hughes	1970-71	Jerry List	1970-72
Dave Humm	1972	Brent Longwell	1971-72
John Hyland	1970-72	Preston Love	1963-64
		Rex Lowe	1969-70

M		Tom Pate	1972
Dan Malone	1970	Frank Patrick	1967-69
Steve Manstedt	1971-72	Glenn Patterson	1967-69
Noel Martin	1962	Jerry Patton	1965-67
Dave Mason	1971-72	Tom Penney	1966-68
Tom McCashland	1970-71	Ed Periard	1968-70
Tom McClelland	1970-71	John Peterson	1971
Kent McCloughan	1962-64	Kelly Peterson	1965-66
Jim McCord	1965-67	Robert Pickens	1966
Donald McDermott	1962	John Pitts	1970-72
Jim McFarland	1968-69	Ronald Poggemeyer	1965-66
Donnie McGhee	1968-70	Ralph Powell	1972
Bernard McGinn	1963-64	Warren Powers	1962
Joseph McNulty	1963		
Lawrence McNulty	1964	**R**	
Harry Meagher	1967	Randy Reeves	1967-69
Wayne Meylan	1965-67	Bob Revelle	1972
Ron Michka	1962-63	Dennis Richnafsky	1965-67
Jeff Moran	1972	Tyrone Robertson	1962
Pat Morell	1970-71	Johnny Rodgers	1970-72
David Morock	1968-70	Paul Rogers	1968-70
Dennis Morrison	1966-67	Terry Rogers	1972
Marvin Mueller	1965-67	Jed Rood	1962
Jerry Murphy	1965	Willie Ross	1962-63
Jerry Murtaugh	1968-70	Steve Runty	1972
		Dick Rupert	1970-71
N		Tom Ruud	1972
Louis Narish	1966		
Bob Nelson	1972	**S**	
Bob Newton	1969-70	Rich Sanger	1971-72
Rod Norrie	1972	Bob Schmit	1972
		Dan Schneiss	1968-70
O		Lynn Senkbeil	1964-66
John O'Connell	1972	Ernie Sigler	1967-68
Bill Olds	1970-72	Lyle Sittler	1962-64
Joe Orduna	1967-68, 70	Bill Sloey	1971-72
James Osberg	1965-66	Maynard Smidt	1963-64
Mike Osborne	1972	Bruce Smith	1963-64
		Frank Solich	1963-65
P		John Starkebaum	1972
Bob Pabis	1970	Dana Stephenson	1967-69
Tom Pappas	1966	Donald Stevenson	1962
Willie Paschall	1962-64	Carel Stith	1965-66

John Strohmyer	1964-65		**W**	
Dennis Stuewe	1962	Larry Wachholtz	1964-66
		Dave Walline	1968-70
T		Bruce Weber	1970-71
Jerry Tagge	1969-71	Wayne Weber	1965-66
Pete Tatman	1964-66	Bob Weinman	1967
Robert Taucher	1965-67	Don Westbrook	1972
Bob Terrio	1970-71	Daryl White	1971-72
David Theisen	1962-63	Freeman White	1963-65
Dennis Thorell	1965-66	Steve Wieser	1972
Bill Thornton	1962	Gale Williams	1967-69
Bob Thornton	1972	Harry Wilson	1964-66
Larry Tomlinson	1962-63	Wally Winter	1968-70
Gary Toogood	1962	Charlie Winters	1965-66
Paul Topliff	1967-69	Bob Wolfe	1971-72
Douglas Tucker	1962-64	Michael Worley	1965
		Keith Wortman	1970-71
U		Mike Wynn	1967-69
James Unrath	1966		
			Y	
V		Zaven Yaralian	1972
Frank Vactor	1969-70	Gene Young	1962-63
Ted Vactor	1963-65		
Lloyd Voss	1962-63		**Z**	
		Mick Ziegler	1966, 68
		Ivan Zimmer	1965, 67

ABOUT THE EDITORS

Francis J. Fitzgerald is a contributing editor to Athlon Sports. A noted researcher and editor, he resides in Washington, D.C.

Jerry Tagge earned all-America honors at quarterback while directing Bob Devaney's Nebraska Cornhuskers to consecutive national championships in 1970 and 1971. He later played professional football with the Green Bay Packers and Chicago Bears of the National Football League.

Now an insurance executive, he resides in Omaha, Neb.